FINDING FREEDOM

Becoming whole
and living free

Books in This Series

When God Seems Silent
Battle Cry for Your Marriage
Finding Freedom
Straight Talk To Leaders

More books in this series coming soon

Experiencing the Supernatural

The TIME Is NOW! Series

FINDING FREEDOM

Becoming whole
and living free

Larry Kreider

Tracie Nanna

Craig Nanna

House To House Publications
Lititz, Pennsylvania USA
www.h2hp.com

Finding Freedom
Becoming whole and living free
by Larry Kreider, Tracie Nanna and Craig Nanna

Copyright © 2017 Larry Kreider, Tracie Nanna and Craig Nanna

Published by
House to House Publications
11 Toll Gate Road, Lititz, PA 17543 USA
Telephone: 800.848.5892
www.h2hp.com

ISBN-10: 0-9987574-0-3
ISBN-13: 978-0-9987574-0-7

Unless otherwise noted, all scripture quotations in this publication are taken from the *Holy Bible, New International Version* (NIV).
© 1973, 1978, 1984 by International Bible Society. Used by permission of Zondervan Publishing House. All rights reserved.

All rights reserved. No portion of this book may be reproduced without the permission of the publisher.

CONTENTS

How to Use This Resource 6
Introduction 9
1. The Cry for Freedom 11
2. The War for Freedom 29
3. Understanding Patterns of Sin and Bondage 49
4. The Power of Forgiveness 69
5. Whose Voice Are You Listening To? 87
6. Healing the Broken Heart 105
7. Receiving the Father Heart of God 125
8. Staying Free 141
Endnotes 162
Teaching Outlines 164
Journaling space for reflection questions 180

How to Use This Resource

Personal study
Read from start to finish and receive personal revelation. Learn spiritual truths to help yourself and others.
- Each reading includes questions for personal reflection and room to journal at the end of the book.
- Each chapter has a key verse to memorize.

Daily devotional
Eight weeks of daily readings with corresponding questions for personal reflection and journaling.
- Each chapter is divided into seven sections for weekly use.
- Each day includes reflection questions and space to journal.

Mentoring relationship
Questions can be answered and life applications discussed when this book is used as a one-on-one discipling/mentoring tool.
- A spiritual mentor can easily take a person they are mentoring through these short Bible study lessons and use the reflection questions for dialogue about what is learned.
- Study each day's entry or an entire chapter at a time.

Small group study
Study in a small group setting or in a class or Bible study group.
- The teacher teaches the material using the outline provided at the end of the book. Everyone in the group reads the chapter and discusses the questions together.

Acknowledgments

As authors, we are grateful to a number of people who made this project possible: Lou Ann Good, for skillful editing; Peter Bunton for reading the manuscript cover to cover and offering valuable insights; Nancy Leatherman for her indispensable expertise as proofreader; and to Sarah Sauder and House to House Publications for making this book become a reality.

Our heartfelt thanks to numerous leaders in the body of Christ and in the DOVE International family who have taught us countless spiritual insights that have helped to shape this book.

Most of all, we give thanks to the God of our Lord Jesus Christ who desires for each of us to become whole and live free.

— Larry Kreider, Tracie Nanna and Craig Nanna

"He went to Nazareth, where he had been brought up, and on the Sabbath day he went into the synagogue, as was his custom. He stood up to read, and the scroll of the prophet Isaiah was handed to him. Unrolling it, he found the place where it is written:

'The Spirit of the Lord is on me,
because he has anointed me
to proclaim good news to the poor.
He has sent me to proclaim freedom for the prisoners
and recovery of sight for the blind,
to set the oppressed free,
to proclaim the year of the Lord's favor.'

"Then he rolled up the scroll, gave it back to the attendant and sat down. The eyes of everyone in the synagogue were fastened on him. He began by saying to them, 'Today this scripture is fulfilled in your hearing'"

(Luke 4:16-21).

Introduction

The struggle is real. We desire to follow Christ, but too often we find ourselves entangled and tripped up, falling back into old patterns of our former selves. The past continues to encroach into our present lives. Why? What is going on?

The writer of Hebrews exhorts us to "throw off everything that hinders and the sin that so easily entangles" (Hebrews 12:1). In this book, we examine how to overcome the hindrances to the life of Christ growing in our lives. We learn from the Scriptures how to find freedom from sin, from lies, from pain and brokenness, and from strongholds the enemy uses to keep us captive.

Jesus came to preach the Good News, promising that the truth will set us free (John 8:32). He came to heal and set free all who are prisoners of sin (John 8:34-36) and oppressed by the devil (Acts 10:38). He came to proclaim and demonstrate the Father's love towards us (John 3:16-17). He came to give us life and life abundantly (John 10:10).

In this book, you will read the stories of men and women who found freedom from sin, from lies, and from oppression of the enemy. They encountered God's love and received healing and restoration. Their lives have been transformed. As authors, we, too, have been transformed. In these pages, we reveal our personal battles to show how God has set us free.

Our prayer is that you find new levels of freedom through reading this book. As you become free and walk in the fullness of life in Christ, you will be able to show others how to find the freedom Jesus promises in Galatians 5:1, "It is for freedom that Christ has set us free."

The time is now to become whole and to live free!

— Larry Kreider, Tracie Nanna and Craig Nanna

CHAPTER 1

The Cry for Freedom

DAY 1: When It All Goes Wrong

My daughter's eyes grew large, reflecting her confusion, fear and hurt as she endured my fury. I (Tracie) knew the words I was shouting at my daughter were hurtful, but I couldn't stop myself. Even as I saw the tears rolling down her face, I continued yelling because I was no longer in control. What was wrong with me?

This event happened the same day that I had resolved to become a "super mom." Because my son Joshua was in the high school musical and had rehearsal every night at 6:00 p.m., family dinnertime had become a real challenge. That day I was determined to give him a home-cooked meal, but my meal preparations were interrupted when Elisa called asking for a ride home from softball practice. This was not the plan. I wasn't supposed to pick her up until 6:00 p.m. My plan for cooking dinner was ruined.

I jumped into the car and tore off to the school. My blood boiled with frustration. When I pulled up to the softball field, Elisa explained that she had misunderstood the coach and practice wasn't finished. I detonated. The target was my daughter. What was going on?

> I knew the words I was shouting at my daughter were hurtful, but I couldn't stop myself.

Was I overwhelmed? Sure. Frustrated? Sure. But where had all this anger come from and so quickly? Why did I seemingly have no control over my words and my emotions?

Was this really about dinner and practice schedules? Could there be deeper issues beneath the surface of my emotions?

Like me, have you ever felt powerless over your actions? Have you ever felt as if something within you is controlling your life? At that time, I was driven by a need to prove to myself and to the world that I was a great mom to my three children. When dinner was sabotaged by softball practice, I retaliated in anger.

Paul describes my dilemma in Romans 7:18-25, "For I know that good itself does not dwell in me, that is, in my sinful nature. For I have the desire to do what is good, but I cannot carry it out. For I do not do the good I want to do, but the evil I do not want to do—this I keep on doing. Now if I do what I do not want to do, it is no longer I who do it, but it is sin living in me that does it. So I find this law at work: Although I want to do good, evil is right there with me. For in my inner being I delight in God's law; but I see another law at work in me, waging war against the law of my mind and making me a prisoner of the law of sin at work within me. What a wretched man I am! Who will rescue me from this body that is subject to death? Thanks be to God, who delivers me through Jesus Christ our Lord!"

REFLECTION
Describe a time in your life when you felt powerless over your actions.

In this passage, Paul is talking about a war going on within us between our sinful nature (flesh) and our inner man (spirit). Shockingly Paul isn't describing someone who doesn't know God. He is talking about a follower of Christ. He is talking about himself—about you and me.

There is a war in each of us between our flesh that has been wounded and trained by sin's effects and our spirit which has been reborn, but needs to learn to trust in and live out of God's love. In this passage, Paul describes the battle that wages, but he also gives us the solution. The key to victory is Jesus. It is Jesus who rescues and delivers us. It is Jesus who offers us freedom from sin and from ourselves. It is Jesus who heals our wounded souls.

Today I am not driven by the fear of not being a good mother to my children; instead, I am motivated by God's love for me and flowing through me. I now trust in the truth that God chose me to mother my three children; no one else can love my children like I can. I also trust that when I fall short, my Father God is well able to pick up the slack. This is freedom!

God desires you to be free as well from the battle between who you long to be and who you are right now.

Wasn't This All Taken Care of at the Cross?

Don accepted Christ in prison. He knew that he was a sinner who needed God's forgiveness. He believed that through the cross, Jesus had paid the price for his sin and that the blood of Jesus cleansed him of all his wrong living. He was born again! He was a new person!

But he was the same person, too. He struggled and fell into the same old patterns, doing the same old things he had done before his conversion. What was going on? Had he not really given his life to Jesus? Was he a hypocrite?

The condemnation Don felt every time he fell short continued to build to the point that Don no longer attended church, read his Bible or prayed. His overwhelming guilt and shame made him feel as if he was a failure as a Christian.

The Bible says that "if anyone is in Christ, the new creation has come: The old has gone, the new is here!" (2 Corinthians 5:17). In Christ, you are a new. This is great news! But how does this happen? Does it happen all at once or is it a process?

> He struggled and fell into the same old patterns, doing the same old things he had done before his conversion.

Is the Gospel only about dealing with our sin? If it is, then we have a list of rules of do's and don'ts to follow. If we obey—we're perfect. If not, we are failures. The Gospel is an invitation to a relationship with God through His Son Jesus. As we journey with God, we can experience restoration in every area of our lives.

Paul said in Galatians 5:1, "It is for freedom that Christ set you free." This freedom is not a fixed point but a line. The line begins when you give your life to Jesus and continues until you see Him face to face. The line is not straight, but curvy, sometimes twisted and jagged. But God is always with us in this journey and He is making something beautiful in it. He is fashioning your life into a masterpiece. "For we are God's handiwork, created in Christ Jesus" (Ephesians 2:10).

Paul speaks of the journey in Philippians 1:6, "being confident of this, that he who began a good work in you will carry it on to completion until the day of Christ Jesus."

REFLECTION
How does your perception change when you understand that salvation is a journey?

Don came to recognize that salvation was the beginning of his journey. He wasn't a "sinner trying to be a saint" but a "saint learning to overcome sin." His identity wasn't in his sin or what he did or did not do, but in whose He was. Most importantly, Don learned that he was not alone on this journey. He was a child of God, loved and accepted by God.

DAY 3

Transformed

Romans 12:2 says, "Do not conform any longer to the pattern of this world, but be transformed by the renewing of the mind. Then you will be able to test and approve what God's will is—His good, pleasing and perfect will."

Conformed has to do with forcing something into a certain shape, a certain way. The Greek word for transform is *metamorphoo*, which means to "change, transfigure, transform," literally from one form to another.[1] It is from this word that we get the English word metamorphosis.

God gives us a beautiful picture of metamorphosis in the transformation of a caterpillar into a butterfly. Inside the cocoon, each cell of the caterpillar literally disintegrates and then reforms into completely new cells of the butterfly. Caterpillars and butterflies not only look completely different, they behave differently as well. The caterpillar crawls, the butterfly flies.[2] The caterpillar lives to eat, the butterfly to reproduce.[3]

> The Bible shows us four things that hinder us.

Change is foundational in order to live for Christ. God expects, requires that we transform from the pattern of this world into the image of His Son (Romans 8:29). We are meant to be a dazzling display of the *metamorphoo*, the transformation of our new birth in Christ.

The life of a Christian, a follower of Christ, is a transformed life. If that is true, why is it so hard? Why is the struggle so great? Sometimes it even feels impossible. Stasi Eldredge explains, "There is a reason. It is found in the life you have lived, the wounds you have received, what you have come to believe about yourself because of them, and not having a clue how to bear your sorrow."[4]

Hebrews 12:1-2 charges us to, "Throw off everything that hinders and the sin that so easily entangles, let us run with perseverance the race marked out for us." There is a course we are to run, the path of transformation, but there are obstacles. Sin entangles and trips us up.

What hinders us? The Bible shows us four things that hinder us. One of those hindrances is generational sin that follow us down our family lineage, the patterns of sin in the families we are born into and grow up in as well as our own patterns of sin we engage in. Another hindrance is ungodly beliefs, the things we believe that are contrary to God's truth, which come from what we are taught growing up, from our experiences and from words spoken over us. Ungodly beliefs are largely formed by a third hindrance; the deep hurts and wounds we have endured. These three hindrances form the last hindrance, strongholds in our lives, which become bondages giving the enemy access into our lives.

REFLECTION
How has God changed your life?

God has a plan for freedom from sin and from each of these hindrances in our lives. This is our hope and promise, "Now the Lord is the Spirit, and where the Spirit of the Lord is, there is freedom. And we all, who with unveiled faces reflect the Lord's glory, are being transformed into his likeness with ever-increasing glory, which comes from the Lord, who is the Spirit" (2 Corinthians 3:17-18).

Put Off, Put On

"You were taught, with regard to your old self, to put off your old self, which is being corrupted by its deceitful desires; to be made new in the attitude of your minds;

and to put on the new self, created to be like God in true righteousness and holiness" (Ephesians 4:22-24).

In the movie, *The Karate Kid*, Daniel is being trained by his karate instructor, Myagi, to defend himself against bullying after being beat up by a gang. Training begins, not by teaching Daniel karate moves, but by having him wax his car. "Wax on; wax off!" he tells Daniel. These movements are foreign and uncomfortable to Daniel and his body aches afterwards, but he is learning the skills that are fundamental to karate, to defend and to defeat attack from his enemy.

> Just as the Karate kid needed to train in order to compete, so must we.

To walk in freedom and victory over the enemy of our lives, we must learn to "put off and put on." This is our training! Colossians 3:9 tells us to "take off our old self with its practices and to put on the new self." There are actions that we will need to stop practicing, and then we must begin to replace them with new actions.

"For we know that our old self was crucified with him, so that the body of sin might be done away with, that we should no longer be slaves to sin—because anyone who has died has been freed from sin" (Romans 6:6-7). Putting off, dying, to our old self brings us freedom from sin.

Galatians 5:16-23 describes this process of "putting off and putting on" in terms of living by the Spirit versus living by the sinful nature or flesh: "So I say, live by the Spirit, and you will not gratify the desires of the sinful nature. For the sinful nature desires what is contrary to the Spirit, and the Spirit what is contrary to the sinful nature. They are in conflict with each other, so that you do not do what you want. But if you are led by the Spirit, you are not under the law. The acts of the sinful nature are obvious: sexual immorality, impurity and debauchery (lustful pleasures), idolatry and witchcraft, hatred, discord, jealousy, fits of rage, selfish ambition, dissensions, factions (divisions), and envy; drunkenness, orgies (wild parties) and the like. I warn you as before, that those who live like this will not inherit the kingdom of heaven. But the fruit of the Spirit is love, joy, peace, patience, kindness, goodness, faithfulness, gentleness and self-control. Against these things there is no law. Those who belong to Christ have crucified the sinful nature with its passions and desires. Since we live by the Spirit, let us keep in step with the Spirit."

REFLECTION
Can you identify what things you need to "put off" as well as "put on"?

Do you recognize the conflict in those verses? Just as the Karate kid needed to train in order to compete, so must we. Allow the Holy Spirit to train you to "put off and put on," and you will win your freedom from sin!

God Wants You to Be Free

DAY 5

A friend once told me, "There is always at least one sin, one thing that everyone struggles with and never truly overcomes." I (Tracie) was a new Christian, but that statement did not sound like God's truth to me, and I told my friend so. At the time, I couldn't quote chapter and verse, but I could not believe that Jesus went to the cross and rose from the dead so that you and I could only partially overcome sin.

Today I definitively know my friend's statement is not true and so does my friend.

1 John 3:8 says, "The reason the Son of God appeared was to destroy the devil's work. For Christ has rescued us from the dominion of darkness and brought us into the kingdom of the Son he loves."

> We now have the power to say "no" to sin in our lieves

What did Jesus win? What did He fight for? Revelation 1:5 speaks of Jesus as the one "who loves us and has freed us from our sins." In 1 Corinthians 15:57 (NLT) we read, "But thank God! He gives us victory over sin and death through our Lord Jesus Christ."

Jesus came to free us from the power of sin and death in our lives. Jesus came to restore our freedom; emotionally, mentally, physically and spiritually. God created us with a free will. This means that He will never force us to do anything we don't want to do. Jesus loves us fiercely and longs for us to love Him back, but He knows true love cannot be forced. He doesn't want our duty: He wants our love. In giving us free will, He gave us the choice to say either "yes" or "no" to Him, to reject or accept Him and His love.

> **REFLECTION**
> *Is there any area of your life, any sin or weakness that you believe you will never overcome?*

Reject Him we did. When sin entered the world, through Adam and Eve's choice, and later, through each of our choices, we are no longer free. Sin entangles us and chains us. Sin takes us where we don't want to go and makes us who we don't want to be. The high price of sin is death; separation from God (Romans 6:23) both in this life and in the life to come.

However, when we have freedom, we are free to choose God. We are free to receive His love for us and free to love Him back. We are free to choose to follow Him and to obey Him. Through freedom, we now have the power to say "no" to sin in our own lives. Oh, how powerful is freedom! We are free to become all that God has created us to be.

In Christ Jesus, you and I were given back God's gift of free will. We are set free so that we can choose freedom. Jesus offers us complete, total freedom and victory over sin and death. My friend discovered the power of his free will, and chose to say "no" to the sin he once struggled with. He chose freedom in Christ and today is walking in that freedom.

Spirit, Soul and Body

"Now may the God of peace make you holy in every way, and may your whole spirit and soul and body be kept blameless until our Lord Jesus Christ comes again" (1 Thessalonians 5:23 NLT).

According to the Bible, we are made up of a spirit, a soul and a body. Our spirit is our "inner man." When we are born again, our spirit is instantly made new (John 3:3-7). This is a done deal that can never be undone. Our spirit is reborn, but our soul and body must undergo a process of becoming holy. God requires us to be "holy in everything we do, just as God who chose you is holy" (1 Peter 1:15 NLT). This process happens through the Holy Spirit working out salvation in our lives, in our soul and body. We cannot do this without the Holy Spirit, but the Holy Spirit cannot do this without our cooperation.

> She was reaching out and grabbing for things in her own way.

Our soul is our mind, will and emotions. The mind thinks and reasons. The will chooses and decides and our emotions feel. Romans 12:2 says, "be transformed by the renewing of your mind."

Our mind must be renewed. We need to learn to think in a new way about everything. Our mind is influenced by the world, but now we renew our minds by the truth of God's Word. We think like Him in order to be like Him.

Jan was a brand-new Christian who struggled in her soul. She continued to think the same way she used to think and therefore fell into doing the same things she used to do. In her heart of hearts, she still believed that she was on her own, and if she didn't make things happen, they wouldn't happen. She was reaching out and grabbing for things in her own way.

In the Bible, we read that Sarah, the wife of Abraham, did the same. God promised her a child, but she didn't really think God would ever make that happen for her so she found her own way to make it to happen. Her way—to have her handmaid bear Abraham's child—was a wrong way that came with negative consequences that continue to affect the world today.

Jan was caught in a cycle that would not change until she renewed her mind to know God's will for her life.

The battle over whether or not we will become like Christ continues in our body. The Bible speaks of the body as "the flesh," our "members," and our "sinful or earthly nature." It is our physical desires, our senses and where our thoughts, choices and emotions are acted out. While renewing our minds is the key to transforming the soul, death is the prescription for our becoming holy and like Christ in our bodies. Yes—death. Death, which is dying to ourselves, is really the only way to become like Christ. Paul says in Colossians 3:2-3, "Set your minds on things above, not on earthly things. For you died, and your life is now hidden with Christ in God." Verse 5 continues: "Put to death, therefore whatever belongs to your earthly nature."

As I (Tracie) write this, I watch in awe as Jan is emerging from the cycle her life was confined to. She is reading and trusting in God's Word and letting it change the way she lives. She is putting to death the old ways and becoming like Christ. It is a wondrous thing to behold!

REFLECTION
What thoughts need to be renewed in your mind?

Freedom from Condemnation

LaVerne and I (Larry) meet many people who are not experiencing true spiritual freedom. Instead they are harassed by condemning thoughts. Let's take a closer look at the spiritual freedom from condemnation, which is available to all believers.

1 John 1:9 says, "If we confess our sins, he is faithful and just and will forgive us our sins and purify us from all unrighteousness."

After we have given our lives to Jesus, the devil may try to paralyze us spiritually by telling us that we are not really saved. Satan is a liar. Despite Satan's accusations, we can know we are saved because the Bible tells us in Romans 8:1-2, "Therefore, there is now no condemnation for those who are in Christ Jesus, because through Christ Jesus the law of the Spirit of life set me free from the law of sin and death." Remember: There is no condemnation to those who are in Christ. The biggest difference between God's conviction and the enemy's condemnation is that God's conviction always brings hope. The devil's condemnation brings hopelessness.

> I got tired of the devil's continual harassment.

The Bible also tells us, "For God is not a God of disorder but of peace" (1 Corinthians 14:33). If your heart is turned toward the Lord and you are still experiencing spiritual doubts and confusion in your life, those thoughts are not from God. The devil is the author of confusion and condemnation. Jesus paid the price on the cross for our freedom.

After I gave my life to Jesus, I continued to struggle with times of intense guilt. One day, I got tired of the devil's continual harassment. I opened my Bible to 1 John 1:9, and declared to the devil, "I'm believing the Word of God that if I confess my sins, He is faithful and just to forgive me of my sins, instead of what I feel in my emotions."

Do you know what happened? I was set free from the oppression of condemning thoughts. Later, I recognized the enemy had placed false guilt over me and was trying to push me into depression, confusion and frustration. But the stronghold of condemnation was broken that day in Jesus' name.

I am reminded of the story about a farmer who was battling with false guilt and confusion in his life. Although he believed in his heart that Jesus had risen from the dead (Romans 10:9), the farmer lacked the confidence of knowing that he was saved. Finally, he went to the back of his barn, took a big stake and hammered it into the ground. He confessed, "Jesus, you are the Lord of my life." Then He made a bold statement. "It happened right here at this stake. I gave my life completely to God. The next time the devil lies to me, I'm coming back here to this stake as proof. From this moment on, I will know, that I know, I am saved!" The farmer made a decision to believe the truth—the Word of God—instead of depending on his feelings. The farmer recognized the false guilt and confusion he was feeling was powerless because Jesus Christ promised eternal life to all who believe. From that day on, life was different for the farmer.

> **REFLECTION**
> *What is the difference between conviction and condemnation?*

You too, can refuse to live under the devil's condemnation. Jesus came to make us completely free! (John 8:32).

Finding Freedom

CHAPTER 2

The War for Freedom

DAY 1

We Are at War

Why is life so hard?

Why do bad things happen?

Why does it feel as if we are fighting an uphill battle?

Actually, it is because you and I are at war.

There is a God—there is a devil—and the battlefield is planet earth. We are in the middle of this war, which is centered on capturing the hearts of men and women. God seeks to win hearts with His love, making us His sons and daughters as Satan seeks to entrap hearts into slavery through sin and death.

The Bible tells us that Satan, who was created by God, led a failed rebellion that resulted in Satan and one-third of the angels being expelled from heaven to earth (Revelation 12:7-9).

> If Jesus triumphed by the cross, why are we still at war?

God also created mankind in His own image (Genesis 1:26, 27) to be the objects of His love and for men and women to love Him in return. Because true love cannot be forced, God gave each of us free will, desiring for us to choose to love Him freely.

Satan took full advantage of this and dealt a brutal blow when he deceived Adam and Eve. Their disobedience allowed sin and death to reign on earth (Genesis 3). But God always had a plan. He sent His one and only

Son Jesus to invade earth to conquer sin and death. "And having disarmed the powers and authorities, he made a public spectacle of them, triumphing over them by the cross" (Colossians 2:15).

If Jesus triumphed by the cross, why are we still at war? Jesus won the victory and has come to lead us to freedom, but we must choose it. He will never force us. The war rages on for our hearts. Who will we choose to follow, to trust, to obey and to love?

This is why Jesus said, "The thief comes only to steal, kill and destroy; I have come that they may have life, and have it to the full" (John 10:10).

This war is between life and death in this world and for eternity. Satan is an enemy of God and therefore is ours also. Satan cannot defeat God, so he goes after the ones God loves—you and me and all mankind. 1 Peter 5:8, "Be self-controlled and alert. Your enemy the devil prowls around like a roaring lion looking for someone to devour."

John Eldredge writes in his book, *Waking the Dead*, "War is not just one of among many themes in the Bible. It is the backdrop for the whole Story, the context for everything else. God is at war.... And what is he fighting for? Our freedom and restoration"[1]

Life is not random, without meaning or purpose. Actually it is full of purpose and meaning, but we often don't understand it. John Eldredge explains it like this, "Until we come to terms with war as the context of our days we will not understand life. We will misinterpret 90 percent of what is happening around us and to us."[2]

One of the battlefronts for me (Tracie) has been in the realm of finances, because finances (or perhaps the lack thereof) have often tempted me to question God's love for me. When I was growing up, my parents went through some extremely difficult times financially and thus began the battle for my heart in this area. Whenever our car broke down, or some other unexpected expense came up, I panicked and questioned God's care for me in the midst of each crisis.

I began to gain ground and to win confidence of God's love when I realized that each crisis

REFLECTION
How does understanding that we are at war help you in your battles?

happens in the context of battle. Satan uses finances to attack my trust in God's love for me, but knowing I am at war, helps me fight accordingly and to win. Instead of giving in to fear and doubt God's care and love for me, I fight back, choosing to place my faith and trust in God who is good and provides for all my needs. With God's help we win. I read the end of the book. We win this war!

DAY 2 Freedom from Demonic Activity

I grew up believing there were demons in Bible times but certainly not in my nation—the United States of America. One night while I (Larry) was teaching a Bible study, a young woman began to crawl around the floor like a snake and a voice began speaking through her that was definitely not her own. I quickly awakened to the reality that demons can control people today.

In the New Testament demons or evil, unclean spirits are mentioned 87 times. According to Derek Prince, the Greek word for "demon possessed" used in the New Testament is best translated "demonized," "to have a demon," or to be "oppressed" by a demon.[3] The Bible tells us that demons are evil spirit beings that are enemies of God and humans (Matthew 12:43-45). In addition, demons can live in the bodies of unbelievers to enslave them to immorality and evil (Mark 5:15; Luke 4:41; 8:27-28; Acts 16:18). Although not all illnesses are the result of evil spirits, demons can cause physical illness (Matthew 4:24; Luke 5:12-13).

> We do not need to fear the powers of darkness.

Jesus' threefold ministry on earth was preaching, healing the sick and delivering people from demons. Acts 10:38 says, "God anointed Jesus of Nazareth with the Holy Spirit and with power, who went about doing good and healing all who were oppressed by the devil, for God was with him."

Jesus said, "If I drive out demons by the finger of God, then the kingdom of God has come upon you" (Matthew 12:28; Luke 11:28). Jesus gave His disciples the same authority to cast out demons (Luke 9:1). In Mark 17:17, Jesus intends for all believers to do the same, "And these signs will follow those who believe: In my name they will drive out demons."

People sometimes ask me if Christians can have demonic activity in their lives. Romans 8:9-11 teaches us that the Spirit of God lives within us and that we belong to Christ. Therefore, as Christians we cannot be demon possessed or under complete control of a demon, but we may be oppressed by demons and demons may influence our thoughts, emotions and actions if we fail to submit to the Holy Spirit's leading in our lives.

People get involved unknowingly with the demonic by dabbling in paranormal energies to gain knowledge of the future or uncover secrets, through things like tarot cards, ouija boards, water witching, seances to contact the dead and drug usage to produce spiritual experiences. All these practices are associated with the occult. Attempting to communicate with the supernatural through these kinds of methods is actually communicating with demons (1 Samuel 28:8-14; 2 Kings 21:6; Isaiah 8:19).

Getting involved in occult practices is dangerous and can lead to demonic bondage. The Bible gives these warnings: "Do not practice divination or sorcery" (Leviticus 19:26). "Do not turn to mediums or seek out spiritists, for you will be defiled by them. I am the Lord your God" (Leviticus 19:31).

I spoke with a Christian leader who told me he had a demon of anger cast out of his life. He had gone through times of uncontrollable anger and didn't understand why he succumbed to anger. Finally one day, he confided in a pastor who took authority over the demon and cast it out in Jesus' name. Jesus Christ set him free. Today that man is one of the most gentle persons that I have ever met.

REFLECTION
Name examples of ways that demons can influence or oppress people today?

Although Satan constantly wars against God's people by trying to draw them away from their loyalty to Christ, we do not need to fear the powers of darkness. 1 John 4:4 (NCV) promises us that we have the victory over Satan and his demons "because God's Spirit, who is in you is greater than the devil, who is in the world."

Overcoming the Enemy

DAY 3

Jesus loved to take His disciples on field trips. Matthew 16:13 records one of those field trips to Caesarea Philippi, to the Gates of Hell or Hades. According to Ray Vander Laan, the Gates of Hell is a large natural cave and was believed to be a gate to the underworld.[4]

It was here that Jesus asks them, "Who do people say I am?" The disciples gave various answers. Jesus presses the point further, "But what about you. Who do you say I am?" Peter declares, "You are the Christ, the Son of the living God" (v. 14, 15).

"Jesus replied, 'Blessed are you, Simon, for this was not revealed to by man, but by my Father in heaven. And I tell you that you are Peter, and on this rock I will build my church, and the gates of Hell, will not overcome it'" (Matthew 16:18). It is at the Gates of Hell, that Jesus makes this declaration. The "rock" that Jesus builds His church upon is the rock of revelation of who He is. This rock of revelation is the foundation of the church and Jesus promises that the gates of hell will not prevail against it.

Revelation 12:11 says, "Now have come the salvation and the power and the kingdom of our God and the authority of his Christ. For the accuser of our brothers, who accuses them before our God day and night, has been hurled down. They overcame him by the blood of the Lamb and the word of their testimony. They did not love their lives so much as to shrink from death."

> I awakened in the night and sensed an evil presence in my room.

How do we overcome Satan, the accuser and enemy of our souls? God has given us spiritual weapons. The first weapon is the "name of Jesus Christ." All authority in heaven and on earth was given to Jesus by the Father (Matthew 28:18). Therefore Scriptures tell us, "that at the name of Jesus every knee will bow, in heaven and on earth and under the earth, and every tongue confess that Jesus Christ is Lord, to the glory of God the Father" (Philippians 2:10-11).

Some time ago, I (Larry) awakened in the night and sensed an evil presence in my room. I was away from home, and no one else was in the house where I was staying. I felt as if I was frozen to my bed. I could only call out the name of "Jesus." Thank God, there is power in the name of Jesus. The evil presence left, and I went back to sleep.

The second weapon the Lord has given to us against the enemy is the "blood of Jesus Christ." I have actually witnessed demons in people who have shrieked in fear at the mention of the blood of Jesus. On one occasion, a man with demons held his hands over his ears and screamed whenever the blood of Jesus was mentioned. The blood of the Lamb frees us from the power of the enemy. We overcome the devil "by the blood of the Lamb."

The third weapon we have been given to defeat the enemy is the "word of our testimony." Our testimony is saying aloud what the Lord has done in our lives and what God is saying about us. We know what God says about us by believing His Word. The truth of God's Word sets us free.

REFLECTION
Who do you say Jesus is?

A few years ago, I met a lady whose son had strayed from the faith. While he was in rebellion, she continued to believe God would speak to him. She knew the Lord had given her a promise in Isaiah 59:21, "My words that I have put in your mouth will not depart from your mouth, or from the mouths of your children." This mother chose to believe God's Word as her testimony. Her son was convicted by the Lord at an unlikely place—a rock concert. Today he is a pastor.

Finally, we overcome Satan when our lives are hidden in Christ (Colossians 1:20). Jesus teaches, "If you try to hang on to your life, you will lose it. But if you give up your life for my sake and for the sake of the Good News, you will save it" (Mark 8:35 NLT). Jesus triumphed over Satan by laying down His life through the Cross. We overcome by submitting our lives to Jesus and the finished work of the Cross.

DAY 4 In the Middle of the Night

Last year, Craig and I (Tracie) took a three-month sabbatical. The first month we went to Cusco, Peru, where we attended language school to study Spanish. Cusco is high in the Andes Mountains and becomes extremely cold at night. Some nights I went to bed dressed with a hat, gloves and two layers of clothing.

Each night, just as we turned off the light, the dogs started barking and fighting. If it wasn't the dogs, it was the cats. If it wasn't the cats, it was the people partying and their loud music. If it wasn't the music, it was fireworks going off at all hours of the night and day. The first time I heard the fireworks, I thought cannons were being fired and we were under siege. I don't think I slept well the entire month because most nights I also conjugated Spanish verbs in my sleep.

One night as I was tossing, turning, half-asleep and complaining about dogs, cats, cold temperatures and verbs,

I heard a voice say, "You can call out to Paccha Mama." Alarmed, I knew the spirit world was battling for my allegiance because Paccha Mama is a spiritual power built upon the beliefs and worship of people living in the Andes Mountains. Craig and I had arrived in Cusco in August, the same month a special festival is dedicated to celebrate and sacrifice to this deity. All our teachers and tour guides made mention of Paccha Mama, whom they also refer to as "Mother Earth."

I share this experience to show that the spirit world is real. Those of us who live in the western world may doubt the existence of evil spirits, but those who live in other parts of the world know better.

> Alarmed, I knew the spirit world was battling for my allegiance.

In the western world and its mindset, we may not give names to the idols and to the powers that we worship and to whom we submit ourselves, but that doesn't make their demonic influence any less real. Devotion to money, position, houses, food, alcohol and prestige can wield the same power in our lives as worshipping a demonic power. The spirit realm is real and it wages war for our hearts.

Paul writes in Ephesians 6:12, "For our struggle is not against flesh and blood, but against rulers, against the authorities, against the powers of this dark world and against spiritual forces of evil in the heavenly realms."

In 2 Corinthians 10:3-5, we are told: "For though we live in the world, we do not wage war as the world does. The weapons we fight with are not the weapons of the world. On the contrary, they have divine power to demolish strongholds. We demolish arguments and every pretension that sets itself up against the knowledge of God, and we take captive every thought to make it obedient to Christ."

REFLECTION
What occupies most of your thoughts, time and resources?

In this passage, Apostle Paul isn't speaking of fighting people with swords but of fighting strongholds built upon thoughts, mindsets and belief systems that are in opposition to the knowledge of God. He explains that we fight by taking thoughts captive, bringing them into submission to Christ.

In the middle of that night in the Andes Mountain, when my flesh was weak, Paccha Mama launched her subtle attack. But my spirit, empowered by the "same Spirit that raised Christ from the dead living in me" (Romans 8:11), was strong. I bolted upright in bed, saying out loud, "I don't think so!" Words of worship and the name of Jesus came forth from my heart. And that was the end of that spiritual battle.

Strongholds

DAY 5

Before my senior year in college, I went on a mission trip to Germany. My teammates and I (Tracie) had the opportunity to tour the Rhine River by boat. Mountains rose up on both sides of the river and dotted along these high cliffs were ruins of ancient castles. These castles not only provided homes for kings and queens, but were also walled fortresses, strongholds, where the people who lived in the surrounding villages could run to for safety from attacking enemy armies.

A stronghold is a place where we run for refuge when we are under attack. In 2 Corinthians 10:4, we read about demolishing demonic strongholds. The Bible also speaks of God being our stronghold. Psalm 9:9 says, "The Lord is a refuge for the oppressed, a stronghold in times of trouble," and Psalm 18:2 tells us, "The Lord is my rock, my fortress and my deliverer; my God is my rock, in whom I take refuge, my shield and the horn of my salvation, my stronghold."

> Karen ultimately met her abuser face to face and forgave him.

A demonic stronghold is a spiritual fortress built by the enemy that stands in opposition to the knowledge of God. Demonic strongholds are built upon areas that Satan has gained access through sin (our own or generationally), through our agreement with his lies and ungodly beliefs and through our hurts (where there is often unforgiveness). A stronghold is where we go to hide when we feel threatened or insecure. They have to do with things we have chosen to hold onto, to trust in, or to lift above God's place in our life. Strongholds keep us from growing in Christ, from knowing God's love and keep us in bondage.

Elisabeth Elliot explains, "Spiritual strongholds begin with a thought. One thought becomes a consideration. A consideration develops into an attitude, which leads then to action. Action repeated becomes a habit, and a habit establishes a 'power base for the enemy,' that is, a stronghold."[5]

Karen sought refuge in alcohol to escape her pain. She had been sexually abused as a young girl. She then believed she was worthless, which led to self-hatred and self-destructive behavior. Now in her forties, she was imprisoned within the walls of this stronghold.

I had the honor of leading Karen to Christ, but for a time, she remained powerless over the hold of alcoholism. Through counseling she received God's healing from the trauma of abuse, replaced the lies with God's truth, repented and received God's forgiveness for hurting herself and others. Karen ultimately met her abuser face to face and forgave him. It was not easy, but she dismantled this mighty stronghold brick by brick. Her life today is not free from struggle, but she has learned that she can run to God and find refuge within the stronghold of His love.

> **REFLECTION**
> *Where do you run to when you feel threatened and insecure?*

Jesus did not only die on the cross for the forgiveness of our sins, but to set us free from strongholds that have been built in our lives. "Thanks be to God! He gives us the victory through our Lord Jesus Christ" (1 Corinthians 15:57).

DAY 6: What Are the Schemes the Enemy Uses in Your Life?

Many of us have vulnerable areas in our lives, which the enemy uses to trip us up in our walk with Christ. Scripture calls these "the schemes of the devil."

"Put on the full armor of God, so that you can take your stand against the devil's schemes." (Ephesians 6:11). The New Living Translation says it like this, "Put on all of God's armor so that you will be able to stand firm against all strategies of the devil." The schemes of the enemy are those strategies of darkness that he uses to pull you down, to bring you into bondage.

> Even though the enemy has a scheme to pull us down, God has a plan to lift us up.

This became clear to me when I (Craig) attended a minister's conference a few years ago. During lunch break, I was sitting at a table with a group of leaders, most of whom I never met before. The woman sitting next to me introduced herself and immediately asked me, "What scheme does the enemy use in your life?"

At first I thought, "Wow, couldn't we start with some small talk first?" I don't think I even answered her, but her question stays with me to this day. I realize that as followers of Jesus Christ, it is essential to "not be unaware of Satan's schemes" (2 Corinthians 2:11) and to be alert to those areas and times in our lives where we are most vulnerable. For you, it may be worry or fear, for others it may be spiritual pride, anger, sexual lust or unforgiveness.

My strengths may not be the same as your strengths, and my weaknesses may not be the same as your weaknesses. My strengths and weaknesses do not make me better or worse in comparison to yours; these just make us human—a human in need of a Savior. You see, the Bible says, "No temptation has overtaken you except such as is common to man; but God is faithful, who will not allow you to be tempted beyond what you are able, but with the temptation will also make the way of escape, that you may be able to bear it" (1 Corinthians 10:13).

REFLECTION
Name the scheme the enemy uses to trip you up in your walk with Christ.

Even though the enemy has a scheme to pull us down, God has a plan to lift us up. It's essential to understand the "scheme" or "strategy" of the enemy against us so that we can be prepared with God's plan to overcome, and call in reinforcements from other strong believers when needed.

Take time to do this short spiritual inventory, and be ready with God's armor so that you can stand!

- What weaknesses and patterns of sin continue to trip you?

- When are you most vulnerable? For most people, it is when we are tired, stressed, alone, etc.

- Do you have a plan in the time of temptation?

- Do you have someone to whom you are accountable?
- Are you in a church or small group that can stand with you in prayer? Don't fight in isolation.

Resisting the Devil

DAY 7

I was driving down the road in my car one day when a spirit of fear enveloped me like a cloud. I (Larry) was temporarily paralyzed with fear, but immediately became aware of what was happening. The enemy was trying to cause me to live by my feelings of fear rather than doing the things I knew God was calling me to do. I proclaimed boldly, "In Jesus' name, I renounce this spirit of fear and command it to leave." Guess what? It left! When we resist the devil, he has to flee! (James 4:7).

A few years ago, I was in Europe and experienced a similar spirit of fear. Again, this spirit of fear had to leave when confronted with the name of Jesus. We do not have to put up with a spirit of fear or any other affliction that the devil will try to bring against us. Jesus Christ has come to set us free.

> If I am really an heir of God, then why do I still deal with depression?

The Bible says, "For God has not given us a spirit of fear" (2 Timothy 1:7 NKJV). If we have a paralyzing fear of Satan and his evil intentions, we are not just fearful; we may harbor a spirit of fear. Satan is the author of fear and wants us to walk in fear. Demonic spirits of all kinds must be resisted and commanded to leave in Jesus' name. We can break the power demons attempt to exert over us. If we are dealing with a violent temper, depression, a sudden compulsion to commit suicide or other life-dominating problems, these may be demonic spirits controlling our lives. We cannot be oblivious to demonic deception. We must be alert to Satan's schemes and temptations, and desire to be set free in Jesus.

To be set free from demonic bondage, we must resist the devil by prayer and proclaim God's Word as we call upon the mighty name of Jesus. A friend told me he sensed a strange, evil presence in a friend's house. Calling upon the name of Jesus Christ, a few Christian believers prayed and took authority over the enemy in that home. The evil presence left. James 4:7 says, "Submit yourselves, then, to God. Resist the devil, and he will flee from you."

Smith Wigglesworth was an evangelist in Great Britain many years ago. He compared the devil to a stray dog that is barking at our heels. He taught that unless we resist the dog, he will continue with his yelping and aggravation. But if we boldly tell him to leave us alone, he will flee. The devil has no choice when we resist him in Jesus' name. He must flee.

As Christians, we can call upon Jesus to defeat Satan and his demonic powers. Matthew 12:28-29 says we can tie up the strong man (Satan) and rob his house (set free those who are enslaved to Satan). "Or again, how can anyone enter a strong man's house and carry off his possessions unless he first ties up the strong man? Then he can rob his house."

We can drive demons out in the name of Jesus by "tying up" the demonic spirit that is influencing our lives or that of someone else's. Only then can we be free. As believers, we can provide deliverance for those who have been held captive by Satan's power. "And these signs will accompany those who believe: In my name they will drive out demons; they will speak in new tongues" (Mark 16:17).

Our God promises us wholeness, emotional health and victory in every area of our lives. "If you belong to Christ, then you are Abraham's seed, and heirs according to the promise" (Galatians 3:29). "The Spirit himself testifies with our spirit that we are God's children" (Romans 8:16).

We are God's children through faith in Jesus Christ. God speaks to us by the Holy Spirit and tells us we are heirs of His promises. He is the God who said He would bless Abraham, and by faith you and I are also the children of Abraham.

You may ask, "If I am really an heir of God, then why do I still deal with depression?" Remember, the New Testament is the new covenant or will that our Father in heaven has left for us. If your uncle dies and wills you his inheritance, you must sign the proper documents to release the inheritance before you can receive it. Spiritu-

REFLECTION
What happens when we resist the devil in Jesus' name?

ally, we must receive our inheritance from God in order to be set free.

We are free when we realize what the Word of God, the Lord's will and our inheritance says, and we act upon it. For example, if you are feeling weak today, claim the strength the Lord promises in His Word. The Bible says, "I can do everything through him who gives me strength" (Philippians 4:13). Confess this promise and receive His strength today.

CHAPTER 3

Understanding Patterns of Sin and Bondage

DAY 1

Sin 101

We know Christ has come to set us free from sin, but what is sin? Three Hebrew words used in the Bible to characterize sin. The most common one is *chata'a*[1], which means "to miss the mark" or "to fall short of the divine standard." This corresponds with the Greek word *hamartano*[2], which appears in Romans 3:23: "For all have sinned and fall short of the glory of God."

A second Hebrew word used for sin is *avon*[3], and means iniquity, guilt or a twisting from or deviation from the divine standard, perversion. The word *avon* is used in Psalm 139:23-24 (NKJV), "Search me, O God, and know my heart; try me and know my anxieties; and see if there is any wicked way in me, and lead me in the way everlasting." *Avon* is translated wicked in English. Wicked means twisted or distorted.

The third Hebrew word we see used for sin is *pesha*[4], meaning "rebellion," "transgression" and "going beyond the limits" of God's law. Pesha describes an attitude of defiance against God. It is used in 1 Samuel 15:23 (NKJV), "Rebellion is as the sin of witchcraft."

> Sin is anything which keeps you from loving God with "all your heart and with all your soul and with all your mind"

All three of the Hebrew words described are used in Psalm 32:1-2: "Blessed is the one whose transgressions (pesha) are forgiven, whose sins (chata'a) are covered. Blessed is the one whose sin (avon) the Lord does not count against them and in whose spirit is no deceit."

God has provided completely for all our sins in Christ Jesus.

Sin is also anything which keeps you from loving God with "all your heart and with all your soul and with all your mind" (Matthew 22:37). Romans 14:23 tells us that anything that "does not come from faith is sin." Hebrews 11:6 builds upon this, "And without faith, it is impossible to please God."

What are the effects of sin? Sin results in the broken world that you and I live in. Sin keeps us separated from God (Isaiah 59:2). It keeps us in guilt and shame, and causes us to try to hide from God and from others (just as Adam and Eve did after they sinned). Sin results in broken relationships, in hurting others and ourselves. It hardens our hearts to God and to others, and leads us to unbelief and being deceived. Hebrews 3:13, "See to it . . . that none of you has a sinful, unbelieving heart that turns away from the living God. But encourage each other daily, as long as it is called day, so that none of you may be hardened by sin's deceitfulness." Sin brings death and destruction (Romans 6:23; Galatians 6:9), both in this life and in the life to come.

In our lives sin leads to bondages. These bondages lead us to sin more and become a vicious cycle. Sometimes we compare ourselves to others whom we believe have sinned much worse than we have, and we tend to excuse ourselves.

This is unwise. We must realize that sin is still sin, and sin can destroy us. If an airplane crashes 200 yards from the runway or 200 miles from the runway, it still crashes and causes destruction.

Here is the promise: "But if we walk in the light, as he is in the light, we have fellowship with one another, and the blood of Jesus, his Son, purifies us from all sin. If we claim to be without sin, we deceive ourselves and the truth is not in us. If we confess our sins, he is faithful and just and will forgive us our sins and purify us from all unrighteousness" (1 John 1:7-9). This verse is spoken to Christians. It implies that we will likely sin. It exhorts us to confess quickly, receive God's forgiveness and cleansing, and continue on in our walk with Christ.

REFLECTION
How would your life change if you truly believed you were forgiven as soon as you confessed your sin to God?

To confess means to say the same thing that God says about something. When we sin, we need to call sin what it truly is: falling short of, turning away or twisting away from God's standard, rebelling against or going beyond God's limits. God promises both to forgive and to purify us when we do. Live a life of confession.

No Desire, No Hook

DAY 2

I have come to realize that the only power the enemy has in my life is what I (Craig) give him. James 1:13-15 says, "When tempted, no one should say, 'God is tempting me.' For God cannot be tempted by evil, nor does He tempt anyone; but each one is tempted when, by his own desire (lust), he is dragged away and enticed. Then, after desire has conceived, it gives birth to sin; and sin, when it is full-grown, gives birth to death."

The progression is this:

Temptation ➡ Desire ➡ Enticed ➡ Sin ➡ Death
　　　　　　　 (lust)　 (by the enemy)

The enemy has no power over us in times of temptation if there is no ungodly desire in our hearts in the first place. It's like this: if someone was to wave a baited hook in front of me using coffee as the bait, I wouldn't bite because I hate the taste of coffee. However, if someone put chocolate on the end of that hook, you would get me every time. When there is no desire, you can't be hooked.

> The only power the enemy has in my life is what I give him.

I believe the enemy is hooking many of us because we are feeding the desire for those things that are against God's will for our lives. Eventually, we can become enslaved to patterns of sin, reaping destructive consequences in our lives. If we continue to feed the offense in our hearts, we will eventually be bound by a root of bitterness that will spring up and defile many. If we continue to feed gossip in the workplace, we will find ourselves in a toxic environment of negativity and backbiting. If we continue to feed the lust in our hearts with pornography, we will eventually be hooked with an addiction that destroys true, godly intimacy in our lives.

James 4:1 says, "What causes fights and quarrels among you? Don't they come from your desires that battle within you?"

It is our unsubmitted desires that give the enemy power in our lives. For this reason, Jesus pointed beyond the action to the condition of the heart because that is where the change needs to begin. "You have heard that it was said, 'You shall not commit adultery.' But I say to you that whoever looks at a woman to lust for her has already committed adultery with her in his heart" (Matthew 5:27-28).

REFLECTION
What desires have you not surrendered to the Lord?

Many of us are trying to grit our way through our Christian walk, trying to not sin, yet our hearts remain unchanged. Jesus wants a surrendered heart because it is from that place everything else flows (Proverbs 4:23).

The Bible says, "Delight yourself in the Lord, and He shall give you the desires of your heart" (Psalm 37:4). Much of our freedom will come not only by kicking the devil out but also by letting the Lord in. I often pray this simple prayer, "Father, take out my desires and give me Your desires." As I delight in Him, my desires shift, and the enemy can no longer hook me.

Wrong Way on a One-Way Street

DAY 3

A few years ago, Craig and I (Tracie) were driving home from visiting family in western Pennsylvania. A few miles after we entered the turnpike, Craig realized we were going the wrong way. We were traveling west when we should have been going east. Craig was convinced that the directional signs to enter the turnpike were wrong. He was so convinced that when we exited the turnpike, he tried to tell the ticket attendant that someone must have maliciously switched the signs at the previous exit.

The attendant, who looked like Rambo, was unconvinced by Craig's claims of sign tampering. It was evident even from behind his reflective sunglasses that he did not care.

Craig, unable to get a refund, paid the ticket and re-entered the turnpike, this time traveling east. Five miles down the road was a huge billboard advertising an airline with the exclamation: "You could have been here by now!"

The Bible also addresses the dilemma between choosing the right and wrong directions. Jesus preached, "Repent, for the kingdom of heaven has come near" (Matthew 3:2). Derek Prince defines repentance as, "an inner change of mind resulting in an outward turning around in a completely new direction."[5] Repentance is realizing you are going the wrong way on a one-way street.

When we repent of our sin, we are choosing to think, feel and say the same thing God does about our actions. Now that we agree with God, we must "turn around" and go in a new direction, turning away from our sin and turning to God. Jesus exhorts us to "Prove by the way you live that you have repented of your sins and turned to God" (Matthew 3:8 NLT). Change of mind, change of heart and change of action are requirements for repentance.

If we have wronged someone, it is necessary to make restitution—ask for forgiveness and make it right if possible. After encountering Jesus, Zacchaeus, a tax collector who had been cheating people out of money, resolved to pay his victims four times the amount he had cheated them (Luke 19:8).

> Craig was convinced that the directional signs to enter the turnpike were wrong.

One Sunday morning at our church, a person gave a prophetic word that someone in the audience had broken the law and was on the run from police. The prophetic word promised that if this person confessed, God would restore him. At the end of the service, a man confessed that he had stolen from several people, including someone in our church. Afterwards, this man turned himself into the police and was convicted to serve a three-year sentence in prison. During his time in prison, he wrote a letter to the man from whom he had stolen and asked forgiveness. Before his release, the man who had committed the theft testified that although he was imprisoned, he was truly free. Acts 3:19 gives a promise to those who repent, "Repent then, and turn to God, so that your sins may be wiped out, that times of refreshing may come from the Lord."

REFLECTION
What does it mean to repent and renounce?

Freedom from sin involves repenting and renouncing. Paul said in 2 Corinthians 4:2, "Rather we renounce secret and shameful ways." Philippians 3:7-8 gives us an understanding of what it means to renounce: "But whatever were gains to me I now consider loss for the sake of Christ. What is more, I consider everything a loss because of the surpassing worth of knowing Christ Jesus my Lord, for whose sake I have lost all things. I consider them garbage, that I may gain Christ."

Generational Sin and Strongholds

One of the things that can hinder us from walking in freedom is generational sin, which is also referred to as "sins of the fathers." These are patterns of sin, passed down from generation to generation. Unrepentant sin can open a spiritual weakness toward a specific sin in a family line, continuing its pattern and strongly influencing future generations.

We read in Exodus 20:5-6, "For I, the Lord your God, am a jealous God, punishing the children for the sin of the fathers to the third and fourth generation of those who hate me, but showing love to a thousand generations of those who love me and keep my commandments."

The word for punish in this verse is the Hebrew word *paqad*, which also means to number or to count.[6] Although God does punish sin, this verse is also saying that God is able to number or count all the times that the sins of the fathers (parents) can be seen in the generations of the children, grandchildren and great-grandchildren in the generations of a family.

Comedian Gilda Radner told a story of a pregnant dog that had her two hind legs cut off by a lawnmower. The dog was taken to the vet, recovered and learned to get around by taking two steps with her front legs and then flipping up her backside. She gave birth to six perfectly formed puppies, but when the puppies learned to walk, they all walked exactly like their mother.[7]

> By the grace of God, I have been free from the generational curse of mental illness.

Just as the puppies learned to imitate their mother, children learn to follow their parents' examples. Children mimic what they see modeled before them, but there is also a spiritual dimension. When patterns of sin are flourishing in the family, spiritual strongholds built upon thoughts and beliefs may cause us to say, "Even God cannot change this circumstance in my life. It's hopeless." We accept this lie and fall into sin that produces a stronghold in our lives.

Multitudes of strongholds can be passed through family lines: addictions such as alcohol, food, compulsive spending; mental problems such as depression, rage, fear; sexual problems such as homosexuality, fornication, pornography; heart issues that include bitterness, greed, rebellion, legalism and gossip; as well as spiritual strongholds, including occult influences.

To be free from generational sins, we confess them to God and repent of them. In Ezekiel 18:14-22, God promises us that we don't have to pay for our family's sins or our sins. When we repent, our sins are wiped away and forgotten.

As I was growing up, I vividly remember various members of my extended family had a history of mental illness. These frightening memories caused me (Larry) to fear that I would become mentally ill and end up in a mental hospital like some of my family members. One day when I was in my early twenties, I became extremely fearful that I was becoming mentally ill. I sensed a deep depression coming over me.

I had been memorizing a scripture verse each day, and one of these verses dropped into my mind. It was Galatians 3:13, "Christ redeemed us from the curse of the law by becoming a curse for us, for it is written: 'Cursed is everyone who is hung on a pole.'" That verse enabled me to realize that I did not need to fear mental illness because Jesus took

> **REFLECTION**
> *Ask the Holy Spirit to reveal to you any generational sin affecting you today.*

the curse of mental illness on the cross for me 2,000 years ago. Since that day, I, by the grace of God, have been free from the generational curse of mental illness.

Although the effects of sin are seen to the third and fourth generation, God promises to show His love to a thousand generations of those who love him and keep his commandments. A choice to turn away from sin does not only affect our own lives but also the lives of our children, grandchildren and our posterity. An icebreaker is a ship that breaks through the ice to make a way for other vessels to follow. Through Christ, we can become spiritual icebreakers and see breakthroughs in our lives and in the lives of our families.

A great example of God's blessing continuing in subsequent generations is evident in the family of Jonathan and Sarah Edwards. Jonathan Edwards was a prominent preacher and theologian in Colonial America. He is associated with the Great Awakening in 1740-1742. He and his wife Sarah had eleven children. By the year 1900, Jonathan and Sarah's descendants included over one hundred overseas missionaries, as well as ministers, professors, educators, authors, judges, lawyers, physicians and holders of public office, leaving an indelible mark on American history and culture.[8] What a wonderful spiritual heritage!

Our actions, both good and bad, affect the generations that follow us. Isn't it exciting to know the freedom that you and I find in Christ will influence a thousand generations in our families?

Ties That Bind

During the past 25 years of ministry, I (Craig) have seen the damaging effects of soul ties in the lives of people:

- Confusion of their identity
- Inability to be intimate with their spouses or be emotionally close to others
- Tormented in their thoughts
- Unhealthy fixation on another person, clouding right judgment
- Continually being drawn back into abusive relationships
- Inability to choose and to obey God

> I feel like a huge weight has been lifted from my life. . . .

How can a "soul tie" have such an effect on a person? It is because a soul tie is an attachment or a bond to another person that ties their souls together, both emotionally and spiritually. The Bible speaks of good, godly soul ties, which have good effects in our lives. For example, the Bible says that "a man will leave his father and mother and be united to his wife and they will become one flesh" (Genesis 2:24).

Marriage is a beautiful, holy soul tie, and so is the tie between a parent and a child, between two friends, between you and God. However the Bible also talks about unhealthy, unholy soul ties that join two people together, resulting in both emotional pain and spiritual bondage. The Bible shares the terrible story when Shechem raped Dinah, and states that "his soul clung to Dinah the daughter of Jacob" (Genesis 34:2-3). The result of this soul tie was that Dinah was "violated." The meaning of that word is "to defile, to hurt, to afflict, to weaken." This does not sound like a good relationship with someone, does it? And this is not God's will for you and me.

A clear comparison between a good, godly soul tie and an unhealthy, unholy soul tie is in 1 Corinthians 6:16-17, "Do you not know that he who unites himself with a prostitute is one with her in body? For it is said, 'The two shall become one flesh.' But he who unites himself with the Lord is one with him in spirit." God desires for each of us to enjoy the benefits of being united with Him and the godly relational boundaries He has set for us, not the destruction that comes through counterfeit connections. These ungodly soul ties can be formed through sexual relationships outside of God's intended purpose between a husband and wife in marriage. They also can be formed by unhealthy, emotional bonds in a close relationship, or in an ungodly vow or commitment made with someone.

The good news is that as you bring these ungodly soul ties to the cross, Jesus can set you free and make you new

REFLECTION
Do you have any ungodly soul ties that hinder your walk with God and hinder you from having healthy relationships with others?

again. After repenting and breaking these ties in prayer, I have heard people say things such as, "I feel so clean… I feel like a huge weight has been lifted from my life… it's like this cloud of darkness no longer is controlling my thoughts and emotions… I feel close again to my spouse—there is nothing separating us anymore."

This result can be for you too! You don't need to be afraid. You don't need to be ashamed. Jesus is greater. I love to tell people that breaking soul ties is much like the doctor cutting the umbilical cord at birth: it doesn't take long, it isn't difficult, but it certainly is a necessity to live!

Breaking the Power of Sexual Bondage

The Bible says, "So God created man in his own image, in the image of God he created him; male and female he created them… God saw all that he had made, and it was very good" (Genesis 1:27, 31). First of all, the Bible shows us in these verses that each of us is created in God's image as either male or female. God has given each of us a clear, sexual identity. Second, who God made us to be was very good. Sex is not bad! Our sexuality is made in the image of God to be very good.

We know that no sin is greater than another, but the reality is that some sins have greater consequences than others. Sexual sin is one of those sins because it is so tied to the core of our identity.

Finding Freedom

Sex is also very powerful. For this reason, the Bible goes on to say in 1 Corinthians 6:18-20, "Run from sexual sin! No other sin so clearly affects the body as this one does. For sexual immorality is a sin against your own body. Don't you realize that your body is the temple of the Holy Spirit, who lives in you and was given to you by God? You do not belong to yourself, for God bought you with a high price. So you must honor God with your body."

> Medical science also proves that God's Word is true.

These verses make it clear that sexual sin affects us. In all the years of ministering to people, I have never had one person say to me (Craig), "Oh, I wish I wouldn't have waited to have sex until marriage." Or, "Oh, I wish I would have had sex with more people." But I've had countless numbers of people saying the exact opposite because of the ongoing effects these sexual ties have left in their lives. Sex is like fire: In the fireplace of marriage, sex brings warmth and comfort to a home; outside of the fireplace, sex will burn the house down!

Medical science also proves that God's Word is true. Multiple reports show that casual sex not only causes multiple sexually transmitted diseases, teen pregnancies, unstable family environments, etc., but it is also harmful to the brain. Dr. Joe McIlhaney and Dr. Freda McKissic Bush in their book, *Hooked: New Science on How Casual Sex is Affecting Our Children,* reveal that the brain chemical oxytocin, a strong bonding chemical (doesn't this sound like a soul tie?), is released into a female's brain during sex. As a result, when a short-term sexual relationship ends, the female is devastated emotionally because she feels bonded to that person. For a male, a bonding chemical vasopressin is released but affects a man in a different way. If a man begins a pattern of having sex with multiple partners, he will risk having the ability to bond at all: it's like tape that loses its stickiness after being applied and removed multiple times.

This scientific study underscores the power of sexual bondage and demonstrates why it is so important to live a life of freedom from sexual sin, including viewing pornographic images accessible today on the internet. Within the holy boundary of marriage between a husband and wife, these bonding brain chemicals will truly bond their relationship and make them "one," but outside of marriage, these chemicals backfire and sexual sin leads to a lot of confusion and brokenness.

REFLECTION
Do you have any sexual bondage in your life?

Paul, in 1 Corinthians 6:9-10, shared a list of things that hinders us from a life in Jesus' Kingdom. Many of those listed are sexual bondages. However in verse 11, Paul made a powerful declaration, "And such were some of you. But you were washed, but you were sanctified, but you were justified in the name of the Lord Jesus and by the Spirit of our God."

Such were some of you! No matter where you are today, or what your past has been, do not be defined by those sexual bondages. You have a new identity; you are made in the image of your Father God and you are now washed, set apart for God, and justified through Jesus Christ!

Putting the Pieces Back Together Again

Tracie and I (Craig) were counseling a young couple preparing for marriage. Both of them loved the Lord, but because of baggage in their past, including previous broken relationships, they continued the same destructive patterns in their relationship with each other.

The couple confessed to us in tears that they were engaging in premarital sex. They knew this action was not what God wanted for their relationship with one another or with Him. After looking at what God's Word said about healthy and holy sexuality, we asked the couple if they wanted to start again and build a relationship God's way. After a wholehearted "yes" from both of them, we led them through a prayer to break previous ungodly soul ties with others, as well as the ungodly soul tie they had with one another.

As I teach others about freedom from sexual sin and from ungodly soul ties, I always like to show listeners a puzzle box cover of Jesus walking hand in hand with a little girl along the beach. The picture illustrates God's plan for each of us—to have an intimate Father-child relationship with Him, a life of holy love. Then I open the box and begin to throw pieces of the puzzle to the audience as I describe the enemy's plan of sexual bondage through sexual abuse, teenage and college conquests, marital affairs, and on and on. This is what the enemy wants—he takes what is pure and holy, and perverts and uses it to bring pain. Before we even realize it, pieces of us are scattered everywhere, and we wonder why we don't feel whole. We cannot feel whole because we have given pieces of ourselves away or others have taken pieces of us away through ungodly, sexual soul ties. But God can restore us again. That's what Jesus did on the cross: He put the pieces back together again. Now we can have that intimate Father-child relationship with Him. We can walk in His freedom of pure, holy love.

> Before we even realize it, pieces of us are scattered everywhere.

A beautiful picture regarding Israel is found in Scripture. I believe this same Scripture speaks to each of us who desire the Father's help in putting the pieces back together after a life of sexual brokenness: "I have loved you, my people, with an everlasting love. With unfailing love, I have drawn you to myself. I will rebuild you, my virgin Israel. You will again be happy and dance merrily with your tambourines" (Jeremiah 31:3-4).

I love that scripture! God calls Israel "my virgin" and assures her that she can be happy again in His perfect, unfailing love. The same is true for you and me today.

Before we closed the premarital session with the couple in our living room that day, we led them through this powerful prayer of becoming whole again, complete in God's love. I encourage you to take time to pray this prayer as well. Allow Jesus to help you put the pieces back together again:

"Lord, through Your Mighty Name Jesus, I renounce and break agreement with every one of these sexual soul ties. I thank You that You are breaking the power of these ties and their influences in my life. These ties will no longer have any hold over me ever again.

"I ask forgiveness for the ways I tied myself with each person (specifically name each person as the Holy Spirit leads). I choose to forgive those who tied themselves to me in ungodly ways. I give back what I took in these unholy soul ties that was not rightfully mine. Lord Jesus, I ask You to bless that person and make them whole again.

I also receive back what was taken from me in each unholy soul tie. Heal me, Jesus, and make me whole again, pure again and holy again in Your Name. I receive Your forgiveness, wholeness and freedom to love you wholeheartedly and to love others in good and godly soul ties. In Jesus' Name, I am whole and I am free!"

REFLECTION
Do you walk in an intimate Father-child relationship with God, and in a life of holy love?

CHAPTER 4

The Power of Forgiveness

Finding Freedom

DAY 1 — Two Men and a Snake

Two men went into the woods to cut down a tree. One man was bitten by a snake. The man was furious and set about to find and kill the snake that bit him. His friend urged him, "Forget the snake! If we leave now, there is time to get you to the hospital and they can save you." But the man would not listen because he was so obsessed in finding and killing the snake. In the forest, the man needlessly died from a snake bite that could have been medically treated and enabled him to live.

> Forgiveness acknowledges the hurt, the pain, the absolute wrongness of what someone did to you and yet realizes that to hold on to unforgiveness only keeps you in a state of pain and bondage.

Author Anne Lamott writes, "In fact, not forgiving is like drinking rat poison and then waiting for the rat to die."[1]

The definition of the Greek word for forgiveness used in the Bible is "to release from bondage or imprisonment; forgiveness or pardon of sins (letting them go as if they had never been committed), remission of penalty."[2]

Simply said, forgiveness means releasing someone of their offense toward you and giving up on seeking payment or penalty for that offense.

Unforgiveness is a trap set by the enemy. Paul said, "I have forgiven in the sight of Christ for your sake, in order that Satan might not outwit us. For we are not unaware of his schemes" (2 Corinthians 2:11-12). He further urges us to "Forgive as the Lord forgave you" (Colossians 3:13).

Here are some truths about forgiveness: God requires forgiveness.

- Forgiveness includes grace; grace is something given which is not deserved; God's grace enables us to forgive.
- Forgiveness acknowledges our merciful Father and enables us to show mercy.
- Forgiveness begins with a choice, an act of our wills.
- Forgiveness acknowledges the hurt, the pain, the absolute wrongness of what someone did to us, yet realizes that to hold on to unforgiveness only keeps us in a state of pain and bondage.
- Unforgiveness keeps us a victim; forgiveness frees us to be able to use our wills to choose.
- There is no justification for the wrong doing someone has done to us, but it helps to understand that hurting people hurt others. We can even begin to pray for that person to experience the love and forgiveness only God can give.
- Forgiveness releases the offender from paying us back and hands the offender over to God to judge, not us.

- Forgiveness sets us free from the tormentor; unforgiveness enslaves us and gives Satan legal access into our lives.

Neil Anderson, author of *The Bondage Breaker and Freedom from Addiction*, writes, "Don't wait to forgive until you feel like forgiving. You will never get there. Feelings take time to heal after the choice to forgive is made."[3]

In Matthew 18, Jesus tells a story about a servant who owed the king one million dollars. He begged the king for extra time to pay the debt. The king had pity on the servant and canceled the whole debt. Then the servant went out and found a fellow servant who owed him two thousand dollars. He grabbed him and demanded immediate payment. The fellow servant pleaded for more time, but the pardoned servant refused and had him thrown into prison.

The king discovered what had happened and called in this servant. "I forgave you a million dollars, but you couldn't forgive someone a few thousand dollars? I showed you mercy, but you could not show mercy to another?"

REFLECTION
Ask the Lord to reveal to you anyone you have not forgiven.

The scripture makes an interesting statement: "In anger his master turned him over to the jailers to be tortured, until he should pay back all he owed. This is how my heavenly Father will treat each of you unless you forgive your brother from your heart" (Matthew 18:34-35). The Lord has forgiven us for so much! Let's receive grace from Him to forgive others as he has forgiven us.

DAY 2

Forgiving God?

"Ascribe to the Lord the glory due His name; worship the Lord in the splendor of His holiness" (Psalm 29:2).

In 1994, Craig and I (Tracie), with our two sons, ages one and two, sold most of our belongings, went through missions training school, and moved to Lima, Peru. A year and a half later, after experiencing the miscarriage of both a pregnancy and of a vision, we found ourselves back in the United States.

I was empty on faith, the mother of two young sons and a precious baby girl. I felt that the Lord had abandoned us while we were in Peru, but my husband was excited to embrace a new beginning and plant a church in a new city. How could I believe that the results would be any different in a new location? I felt that praying to God was like playing a game of chance. How could I trust that God would answer our new prayers since He had not answered our earlier prayers?

> Forgive God?
> You may ask, how does He need forgiveness?

But the Lord is faithful, even when we are faithless (2 Timothy 2:13). One day as I was pouring out my anger and hurt, I realized that I needed to forgive God. Forgive God? You may ask, how does He need forgiveness? He is perfect! Yes, He is, but we need to understand, forgiveness isn't for the other person, it is for ourselves.

I was angry at God because He had allowed me to walk through a valley of pain when I wanted Him to keep me out of it. He could have prevented it, I reasoned. As I chose to forgive God and the weight of bitterness lifted, I could, in retrospect, see how God's glory and His goodness had visited me and how He walked me through and even carried me in that valley. When I "forgave" God, I felt again His love for me. He had never left me.

I began to meditate and chose to believe the verses found in Psalm 62:11-12, "One thing God has spoken; two things I have heard: that you, O God are strong, and that you, O Lord, are loving." I determined to believe who God says He is instead of allowing my experiences and feelings to dictate for me God's heart and character. Again and again, I remind myself that God is strong enough to carry me through whatever comes my way and His love for me will never end.

REFLECTION
Is there anything for which you need to "forgive" the Lord?

Anger and Forgiveness

"[Love] is not easily angered. It keeps no record of wrongs" (1 Corinthians 13:5).

Craig asked me (Tracie) to forgive him. It was for something I had held on to for many years. I knew I needed to forgive him. God required that I forgive him. However, in order to do so, I would need to give up my anger toward him. I could not do that. I was not ready to say, "I forgive you."

Why didn't I want to forgive? One reason is that I did not want to give up my anger. Anger follows hurt and injustice. I reasoned that letting go of anger would nullify my pain.

I believed my anger was my justice. It was the wall around my heart. Anger alone protected me. Anger alone acknowledged my pain, my hurt. Only anger saw me cry. Anger was the amplifier to my voice. My fears, my thoughts, my concerns, my feelings, my pleas, my desperate cries were lost in the wind without anger to give them volume. Anger was the only power I had, the only thing with which I could control my world.

But anger is a master, not a servant. I had used anger to control my surroundings, but anger was controlling me. My anger inflicted pain on those I loved. I had miscalculated the price anger demands.

> I can kick anger right back out, the same way I let it in.

I knew that to truly forgive, I needed to end my alliance with anger. I had been deceived in believing there was peace with anger. Realizing the truth, I chose to turn my back on anger. I chose to forgive. I chose to forgive as the Lord forgave me (Colossians 3:13). I also chose to trust God with my heart and with my pain.

Finding Freedom

I remember clearly the day I told Craig as we were sitting in a restaurant that I had chosen to forgive him. I told him that I was no longer going to attempt to manipulate him into hearing me and giving me what I thought I needed. I was no longer going to use my anger as a weapon. I was going to trust that God would speak to him and work in his life. I promised Craig that I would choose daily to forgive and love him even if I thought he did not deserve it.

REFLECTION
What is the hardest thing for you about forgiving someone?

In that moment, our relationship did not automatically become perfect, but something profound changed in me. Because I renounced anger and chose to forgive, anger no longer had the same power over me. That is not to say that I never feel angry or hurt; I do. However, anger is no longer smoldering within me. Oh, it knocks on the door. Most of the time I am wise enough not to open the door. But even in my weakest moments when I do let anger in, I can kick it right back out, the same way I let it in. Anger is no longer a resident in my soul, but an unwanted visitor. I am free.

The Power of His Grace

DAY 4

When we experience the grace of God, tremendous spiritual power is released that gives us freedom. Grace is the free unearned favor of God on those who do not deserve it—that is us!

Years ago, we (Larry and LaVerne) were involved in a youth ministry. Coming home one day, we discovered that someone had thrown a big rock through our window. We knew the rock-thrower was someone we cared about and to whom we had ministered. Instead of pursuing charges against the vandal, we extended grace. The Lord helped us to take the attitude that it was only by His grace that our whole house did not have every window broken! We could have cried and complained and (gotten stuck) become bitter, but God's grace gave us the power to forgive, bless and continue to build His life in the people whom He had placed in our lives.

Grace is also the power and desire to do His will. 1 Peter 5:5-6 says, "God opposes the proud but gives grace to the humble. Humble yourselves, therefore, under God's mighty hand, that he may lift you up in due time."

> Healthy people practice self-talk.

Humility is an attitude of total dependence on Jesus Christ. Pride is the opposite of a healthy understanding of the grace of God. The Scripture makes it clear that if we humble ourselves under the mighty hand of God, He will exalt us in due time.

God wants to exalt you. He wants to honor you. When are we honored by God? When we humble ourselves before Him. If I try to do God's job, if I try to exalt myself, then God needs to do my job. He would need to humble me.

I would rather humble myself and allow God to exalt me than have God humble me, wouldn't you?

Humility places us in the position to receive this grace. True humility is constantly acknowledging that without Jesus we can do nothing, but with Jesus we can do all things.

We have found that healthy people practice self-talk. Don't be afraid to talk to yourself. Speak words of grace to yourself. I talk to myself all the time. The real issue, however, is what do we say when we talk to ourselves? If we speak words based on fear and worry, the words induce harm. If we speak words of truth and life and grace to ourselves, the self-talk will keep us healthy both spiritually and emotionally.

REFLECTION
What is a definition of grace?

The Bible says David talked to himself; he "encouraged himself in the Lord" (1 Samuel 30:6 KJV). We should be doing the same thing. I encourage you to get up in the morning and say, "I am right with God today through faith in Jesus Christ. I am a man or woman of God. I can do all things through Christ who strengthens me today" (Philippians 4:13).

Let's speak life and live in health today!

It's All Grace

Sam worked hard at being a Christian. If Jesus was willing to suffer and die on the cross to pay for his sins, Sam believed he owed God nothing less than his very best. But Sam grew tired, exhausted and frustrated. When he could not make any significant dent on paying his debt to God, Sam gave up and went back to the way of the world.

The book of Galatians was written for all who struggle as Sam did. If we are honest, don't we all struggle at times?

"You dumbies! Who tricked you?" Paul asks. "You were running a good race—who cut in on you? What are you doing!" (Galatians 3:1; 5:7). Galatians 3:2-5 tells us, "I would like to learn just one thing from you: Did you receive the Spirit by the works of the law, or by believing what you heard? Are you so foolish? After beginning by means of the Spirit, are you now trying to finish by means of the flesh? Have you experienced so much in vain—if it really was in vain? So again, I ask, does God give you his Spirit and work miracles among you by the works of the law, or by your believing what you heard?"

What is your salvation based on: your works or faith?

> What would a church filled with people extending grace to each other look like?

Ephesians 2:9, tells us that "it is by faith you have been saved, through faith–and this not by yourselves. It is the gift of God–not by works, so that no one can boast." We know that verse; we agree with its premise. We definitely need God's grace to be saved. But that is only a start. Then what happens? Are we on our own, needing to prove we are saved by behaving perfectly? Needing to be good so we stay saved?

We are saved by grace, but too often, we try to live the remainder of our life on our own. Paul says to us in Galatians 5:1 (NLT), "So Christ has truly set us free. Now make sure that you stay free, and don't get tied up again in slavery to the law."

John Bevere tells of a survey taken in 2009 of 5,000 Christians across America.[4] They were asked to give three or more definitions or descriptions of grace. Ninetyeight percent answered that grace was salvation, God's unmerited gift and the salvation of sin. Only 2 percent said grace was empowerment. Bevere went on to say, "If only 2 percent of Christians know that grace is God's empowerment that gives me the ability that goes beyond my natural ability, that means that 98 percent of Christians are trying to live holy in their own ability."

REFLECTION
What is your salvation based on, your works or faith?

God told Paul in 2 Corinthians 12:9 NLT, "My grace is all you need, for my power works best in your weakness." Paul concludes, "So now I am glad to boast about my weaknesses, so that the power of Christ can work through me." Weakness is our own human inability. God doesn't seem shocked by our weakness. He knows all about it and has a plan. The plan is His grace. Grace is God's ability to do what we cannot do in our own strength. That is good news!

Instead of trying to hide our weakness from God and others, what if we offered it to God in exchange for His grace? What if I accepted others' weakness and encouraged them to do the same? What would a church filled with people extending grace to each other look like?

I am delighted to tell you that Sam has come back to the Lord, is being discipled by someone in our church and is learning that he doesn't need to do it all himself. He is beginning to boast in his weakness and live by God's grace.

DAY 6
Letting Go to Reach Upward

"Not that I have obtained all this, or have already been made perfect, but I press on to take hold of that for which Christ Jesus has taken hold of me . . . Forgetting what is behind and straining toward what is ahead, I press on toward the goal to win the prize for which God has called me heavenward in Christ Jesus" (Philippians 3:12-14).

The summer between my junior and senior year in college, I (Tracie) went on a mission trip to Germany. In preparation for this trip, participants attended a training camp. One of our activities required us to climb a thirty-foot climbing wall. We were in a harness and attached to a partner with a rope and belays, but thirty feet felt like a thousand to me.

> Climbing the wall is a lot like life.

Attached to the wall were various handholds and footholds for us to grab hold of while ascending to the top. The holds were far enough apart that in order to proceed upward, we needed to take one hand and one foot off the perspective holds in order to reach forward for the next holds. For each millisecond we did this, we were fully aware that we were vulnerable to fall.

We had to look up, choose our next handhold and foothold and reach upward. It was not as much physically difficult as it was mentally difficult to keep from looking down or from letting go while reaching up to grasp the next secure hold. We also had to trust that our partner was paying attention and would prevent us from falling to the ground if we lost our grip and slipped. This feat became more and more difficult the higher we climbed. But each time we repeated the process of letting go and reaching upward, we got closer and closer to our goal—the platform at the top of the wall. Not everyone made it. Some people became paralyzed by their fear and had to be helped down.

My roommate Beth did not climb the wall only one time, but she chose to do it a second time—blindfolded. Without her sense of sight, she reached upward again and again, feeling for the handhold and foothold she trusted was there. She was fearless and made it to the top!

Climbing the wall is a lot like life. In order to "take hold of that which Christ took hold of us," we need to let go—let go of our past mistakes, our hurts, our unforgiveness, our offenses and our sin. We must let go in order to obtain the freedom that God has for us. Let go and reach upward. . . . There is no other way to reach the goal of heaven. We must also trust that our partner—God—is holding the other end of the rope, that we are forever attached to Him and that He will never, ever let go of us. We cannot become paralyzed by fear to obtain freedom.

The Israelites had to let go of Egypt to reach the Promised Land. Sadly, many of them choose not to let go and died after wandering in the desert for forty years.

Even Jesus needed to let go of His desires to achieve the goal for which the Father destined Him. In His years on earth, Jesus prayed to his Father, "Not my will but your will be done" and "for the joy that was set before Him endured the cross . . . and has sat down at the right hand of the throne of God" (Philippians 2:12 NKJV).

REFLECTION
What are the consequences of not letting go?

Finding Freedom from Painful Memories: The Bell Theory

DAY 7

Many years ago, a Christian leader circulated a letter to other leaders in our church that questioned my character. I (Larry) felt helpless in proving my innocence. I tried to claim God's promises, but nothing seemed to help. The voice of the accuser grew stronger in condemning me for everything that was wrong; convincing me that all God had done in my life was ending in shambles. I questioned why God did not rescue me from vicious accusations. Why did God seem to forsake me during these dark hours in my life?

The Good News is that God did not leave me. He promises in Hebrews 13:5, "Never will I leave you; never will I forsake you." I learned He really keeps that promise! He was with me constantly, working in ways I did not comprehend at the time. I learned that God does indeed work in our lives, deep beneath the surface, even in the midst of our pain. But I still needed to find freedom from the painful memories I carried.

> I could still remember the incident, but the painful emotions were completely erased.

I knew I must forgive, but I needed help. Eventually, I went to a friend whom I trusted and to whom I opened my heart. He encouraged me to forgive in Jesus' name all who had hurt me. My friend prayed that I would receive emotional healing from painful memories. I found strength to go on, but to my dismay the painful emotions did not disappear immediately even though I had forgiven the one who offended me and received prayer as instructed in James 5:16, "Therefore confess your sins to each other and pray for each other so that you may be healed. The prayer of a righteous person is powerful and effective."

At first I was perturbed that complete healing did not happen immediately. Then I read that Corrie ten Boom, who experienced the horrors of a Nazi concentration camp and whose life story inspired the movie, *The Hiding Place*, often compared emotions and memories to "the ringing of the church bell." A church bell clangs loudly whenever someone pulls the long chord attached to the ringer, but when the ringer stops pulling the cord, the reverberations grow softer and fainter until the sound ceases completely.

Corrie said that whenever you forgive someone who has hurt you, some of those old emotions of hurt and pain may surface again and again. That is the time for us to say emphatically, "In Jesus' name, I know He took my pain on the cross." As we declare this truth, the emotions of hurt feelings dissipate. We learn to focus on Jesus our healer instead of on the pain. In the same way that the sound from the church bell rings loudly at first and then becomes fainter, the painful emotions will fade until we are completely healed from the stinging pain attached to the memories.

REFLECTION
Do you struggle with painful memories? Are you ready to be set free?

Whenever the painful memory surfaced in my thoughts, I verbally reminded myself, "I already forgave and received healing of these memories—I am free in Jesus' name." The memories lessened every day until the painful turmoil they provoked was gone. I could still remember the incident, but the painful emotions were completely erased. Instead, I strongly sensed the grace and healing of God in that area of my life.

About ten years after this leader sent the letter of accusation to various leaders in our church, he took me out for breakfast and asked me for forgiveness for accusing my character to other leaders. I thanked him and told him that I had already forgiven him years before. In looking back, I am so grateful I was already free from the painful memories. Some people think someone must admit the wrong they have committed against them in order for them to be set free, but this is not the case. Someone admitting they were wrong can be a fringe benefit, but we can find freedom even if they never admit their wrongdoing. We are not set free because someone confesses his or her wrongdoing. Jesus is the one who sets us free.

God will also set you free as you forgive in Jesus' name, receive His healing from the painful memories and daily thank Him for what he has already done in your life. The bell theory will help you experience complete freedom from painful memories.

CHAPTER 5

Whose Voice Are You Listening To?

Whose Voice Will You Follow?

DAY 1

I (Tracie) played basketball growing up. My dad was my greatest coach and my greatest cheerleader. My junior year I played on the varsity team. During one game, I had the ball and as usual was trying to drive with my left hand. That technique generally worked well for the first five minutes of the game until my defender figured out how very left-handed I was and started defending me accordingly.

My dad yelled from the stands, "Drive with your right hand!" I stopped in the middle of that game, looked up at my dad and yelled back to him, "I'm trying!" After the game I walked up to my dad (I had to because he was my ride home), sheepishly looked at him and told him I was sorry. He sheepishly told me he was sorry, too. Neither of us said much on the ride home.

When you play a sports game, there are voices you need to listen to and those you need to shut out. That night, I learned that I needed to train my ear to hear my coach's voice over all other voices—the crowd's and even my dad's during the game. But after the game, I continued to ask my dad to talk over the game play by play.

The Lord taught me through this experience that it is the same with life. We must train ourselves to listen to God's voice above all others. We must shut out the enemy's voice and all his accusations, lies and condemnation. We must be able to pick out our Father God's voice among the many voices in the crowd.

How do we know God's voice? My dad has a unique voice. People say he sounds like Bosley on the show "Charlie's Angels" (1970s throwback). I can recognize my dad's voice anywhere. I don't recognize God's voice as much by what He sounds like but by the words His voice says.

One who is trained to detect counterfeit money isn't trained by studying the counterfeits but by studying money which is authentic. This person knows the genuine so intimately that he can easily spot counterfeits.

We train ourselves to know God's voice by studying His Word. Paul exhorts us to "Do your best to present yourself approved, a workman who doesn't need to be ashamed and who correctly handles the word of truth" (2 Timothy 2:15).

> There are voices you need to listen to and those you need to shut out.

We learn His ways and His character from His Word. For example, "I've learned about God's love from 1 Corinthians 13. I've learned that His wisdom is "first of all pure; then peace-loving, considerate, submissive, full of mercy and good fruit, impartial and sincere" (James 3:17). I've learned that He is "compassionate and gracious, slow to anger, abounding in love" (Psalm 101:3).

I know God's voice because I know His words. I know what He may say and what He will not say. I know Him intimately through spending time with Him in prayer and in His Word.

Jesus taught in John 10:4-5 that the sheep follow the shepherd "because they know his voice. But they will never follow a stranger . . . because they do not recognize a stranger's voice." Jesus is the Good Shepherd and in order to follow Him we must know His voice.

> **REFLECTION**
> *How can you learn to recognize God's voice?*

Mirror, Mirror on The Wall

DAY 2

While visiting with Larry's wife, LaVerne, she pointed to the new mirror on her wall. Noticing the attractive silver frame, I (Tracie) told her it was very pretty. "No, look in the mirror," she said. I looked again, this time into the mirror. Whoa! The reflection was distorted, like those crazy mirrors at the carnival. You know the ones, where you look completely misshapen. The mirror was defective. LaVerne told me she was going to return the mirror for a new one.

> Our mind can distort things and reflect things incorrectly, causing us to see things wrong.

Our minds can be like that mirror. Our minds can distort things and reflect things incorrectly, causing us to see things wrong. Dead wrong.

The heart, which is referring to our thoughts and our emotions, is described in Jeremiah 17:9, as being, "deceitful above all things and beyond cure. Who can understand it?"

Let me say that God understands our hearts and can truly cure all our heart's pain—we'll talk about that later.

But the point Jeremiah is making is that our hearts, our thoughts and emotions can lie to us, they do this all the time.

That is why we jump to conclusions like I did on my eighteenth birthday. I wanted to hang out with my friends but everyone told me they were busy. The whole week before my birthday, my friends stopped talking whenever I walked into the room. I noticed them often whispering behind my back. I felt as if I did not have a friend in the world . . . until I walked into my house and thirty friends screamed, "Surprise!" My earlier assumptions had been completely wrong. My parents and friends loved me. Their busyness, whispering and conspiring happened because they loved me enough to throw a surprise party for me.

Why do we so often jump to wrong conclusions? Because we filter everything we see, hear and feel through our flawed thoughts and emotions. I refer to these wrong conclusions as lies or ungodly beliefs because they are contrary or in opposition to God's Word, His nature and/or His character.

REFLECTION
Can you identify any ungodly beliefs through which you are filtering life?

Ungodly beliefs come from several sources. Satan is the master crafter of ungodly beliefs and Jesus referred to the devil as a "liar and the father of lies" (John 8:44). Ungodly beliefs also come from the world around us. That is why we are told in Romans 12:2, "do not be conformed any longer to the pattern of this world but be transformed by the renewing of your mind." We form ungodly beliefs from what we have experienced and through words spoken over us by others and even ourselves.

These ungodly beliefs affect how we view God, how we view ourselves and others, and how we view the world around us. An unrenewed mind causes us to question the following:

- Is God good? Does He care about me?
- Do I have value? Does anyone value me?
- Am I loved? Am worthy of being loved?
- Are people safe? Is the world safe?

Our answers to these questions affect our entire lives. You and I need a new mirror, a new filter.

"I pray that you, being rooted and established in love, may have power, together with all the Lord's holy people, to grasp how wide and long and high and deep is the love of Christ, and to know this love that surpasses knowledge—that you may be filled to the measure of all the fullness of God" (Ephesians 3:17-19).

Who Do You Think You Are?

I (Tracie) was out of town at a conference to receive—freedom. One night in the hotel room, I tossed and turned, unable to sleep. In two weeks, I was scheduled to preach in our church. It was one of the first times I had ever preached. I was replaying my message in my mind but was constantly being interrupted by thoughts such as: "You don't have anything important to say," "no one is going to be interested in that," "you don't have the anointing or gifting to preach." Then came the final blow: "Who do you think you are?"

I bolted upright in bed, went to the bathroom, turned on the light and said, "In the name of Jesus—devil, shut up. I am a nobody, but I am a child of God. He chose me, and I am His." I went back to bed and slept well the remainder of the night.

Satan's name literally means "accuser." He went before the throne of God and accused Job. He also accused the high priest Joshua in Zechariah 3:1-7. "The Lord said to Satan, 'The Lord rebuke you Satan! The Lord, who has chosen Jerusalem, rebuke you! Is not this man a burning stick snatched from the fire?' Then He said to Joshua, "See I have taken away your sin, and I will put rich garments on you."

> Who do you think you are?

You see, Joshua was the high priest during the time when many Israelites were allowed to return to Jerusalem after exile in Babylon. They were to rebuild the temple and the city of Jerusalem. It was during the attempt to do this that Satan tried to destroy Joshua by accusing him of his sin.

Often when you and I attempt to step out in faith in obedience to God, Satan accuses us. In that moment, we need to know who we are in Christ Jesus. We need to be able to differentiate between God's voice and the voice of the accuser. How can we discern whose voice we are hearing?

Satan is one hundred percent consistent. He continually seeks to accuse and condemn you. God never condemns, but He will convict. What is the difference? Condemnation sounds like this: "You are a sinner, and you will always be a sinner. You will never change. You are hopeless. You might as well just give up."

When we hear God's conviction we will hear, "Yes, you sinned, but you are forgiven. It is not who you are. You are my child. You can do this. I will be with you always."

REFLECTION
How can you discern the difference between condemnation and conviction?

Romans 8:31-34 (NLT), "If God is for us, who can ever be against us? Since he did not spare even his own Son but gave him up for us all, won't he also give us everything else? Who dares accuse us whom God has chosen for his own? No one—for God himself has given us right standing with himself. Who then will condemn us? No one—for Christ Jesus died for us and was raised to life for us, and he is sitting in the place of honor at God's right hand, pleading for us."

DAY 4
Stop Believing the Lie and Start Speaking the Truth

This past year, I (Craig) got a crazy idea to do a triathlon. Let me be clear, it was a sprint triathlon (500 yard swim, 16 mile bike and a 3.1 mile run)—not a full Olympic triathlon—but it was still a triathlon and it was no joke! I had spent months in training, but a week before the actual triathlon, a lie began to play over and over in my head: "You don't have what it takes to be an athlete."

I had heard those words before. You see, when I was in junior high, I ran track for my school. At the first meet, I ran the 400m and came in dead last. Afterwards my grandfather came to me, shook his head and said, "You just don't have what it takes to be an athlete." From that point on, I never joined another organized sports team. I accepted my grandfather's words as my truth. I accepted a lie that came to haunt me more than thirty years later.

> I accepted a lie that came to haunt me more than thirty years later.

This example shows why it is important that we are careful what we speak—to others and to ourselves—especially to young, moldable lives that are so vulnerable to an adult's assessment. Proverbs 18:21 says, "Death and life are in the power of the tongue, and those who love it will eat its fruit."

Lies often become ungodly beliefs in our lives that contradict God's truth, God's Word, and God's heart toward us. Ultimately these lies come from the devil, "for he is a liar and the father of lies" (John 8:44). Satan uses these lies to form belief systems that affect our behavior, our decisions, and our relationships. When these lies begin to replay in our minds, the Bible says that we can know God's truth, and it's His truth that will set us free from the continual damaging effects from these lies (John 8:32).

When I began to hear that lie the week before my triathlon, I also heard the voice of God's Spirit say, "I want you to begin to declare, 'I am an athlete, and not only an athlete, I am a triathlete.'" At first I felt ridiculous speaking that declaration because I have never considered myself very athletic. However, as I followed God's voice and began to speak His truth, something changed deep inside me. I realized that this was not just about a triathlon, but this was about God redefining me according to His Word and not by what others spoke over me.

Sure enough, on race day, I finished the race. I finished strong because God's truth within me produced different results.

REFLECTION
What is God's truth to replace that lie and set you free?

DAY 5

The Power of Words

Through tears Jennifer shared that she was struggling with receiving love from her husband. He was a good man who truly loved her. They had a beautiful family, but she did not feel deserving of her husband's love and could not fully trust his love for her.

I (Tracie) asked her if she could identify the source of her struggle. She shared that when she was about twelve years old, a neighbor boy had told her she was so ugly that no man would ever want her.

Words are powerful. In Genesis God spoke and the world came into being. Words carry the power of death and life. In James 3:10 we read, "Out of the same mouth come blessing and cursing. My brothers, this should not be. Can both fresh water and salt water come from the same spring?"

No, it should not be. I wish everyone could skip adolescence, a time of insecurity as we awkwardly attempt to grow into ourselves. Jennifer was so vulnerable to this verbal attack and the words struck deep into her heart. Those words whispered accusingly to her for the next decade. To her those words were true and nothing her husband or anyone else could say changed her mind. She had a husband who loved her, but she was closed off to his love because she believed he either wasn't sincere or he was blind and any day now he would realize his mistake in choosing her.

We spent a good deal of time in prayer, and I asked her to do several things. I asked her to forgive the boy who had spoken, those cruel words. I asked her to repent from agreeing with those words and to break agreement with those words. I asked her to repent of rejecting her husband's love for her and for judging him for loving her. Then we asked Jesus to heal this hurting, broken place of her heart and to speak truth to her. Jesus was so faithful! He did speak to her, and His truth replaced the lie she had battled for so long.

> Replace the lies with God's truth.

Jeremiah 31:3 says, "I have loved you with an everlasting love; I have drawn you with loving-kindness. I will build you up again and you will be rebuilt." This is what God did for Jennifer that day and what He desires to do for each of us.

Words have great power. They can tear us down and they can build us up. Jesus has come to speak truth in our lives to dispel the lies that we have come to agree with and believe about God, ourselves, people and the world we live in. Jesus said in John 8:32, "Then you will know the truth, and the truth will set you free."

We must replace the lies with God's truth. His truth is found in His Word. When Jesus was tempted by the devil in the desert, He resisted with the Word of God. Ask God to speak truth to you and search the Scripture for His truth. Write down His spoken and written words, memorize them and use them to overcome the lies. These words are your victory and your freedom.

REFLECTION
Have these words turned into lies that you have accepted as truth?

DAY 6: Whose Report Will You Believe?

Jerry was in his mid-twenties, married with a new baby girl, when he had his first seizure. After many tests, doctors did not give him a good report. They told him that the seizures were causing lesions on his brain and that he would most likely not live beyond fifty years of age. While Jerry and his wife fought to trust God for health, the doctor's diagnosis hung around his neck like a chain and whispered that he would not be there to walk his daughter down the aisle, see his son grow up to be a man, become a grandpa or grow old with his wife.

God has promises and purposes for our lives. God promises us in Jeremiah 29:11, "For I know the plans I have for you," declares the Lord, "plans to prosper you and not to harm you, plans to give you hope and a future."

Satan also has a plan, but his is for our destruction. His very name means "accuser." We read in the Bible that he went before the throne of God to accuse both Job and the high priest Joshua (Zechariah 3). Two plans and purposes are laid out for our lives: one from God, and one from Satan. We are warned in 1 Peter 5:8 to, "Be alert and of sober mind. Your enemy the devil prowls around like a roaring lion looking for someone to devour."

> Two destinies warred within him.

For twenty some years, two destinies warred within Jerry. Jerry pastored and ministered in his church, his community and went to Haiti countless times to minister even while having seizures almost daily. He fought to push forward to see his God-given dreams and vision come to pass even as he warred against the enemy's plan for him to die young, leaving his wife and children without a husband and father.

Praise be to God, last year when Jerry was forty-five years old, he went through a new series of tests. The brain scan showed only a few lesions on his brain and the doctor told him that the scarring on his brain was so minimal that it would never be the cause of death in his life. Doesn't a different report change everything?

God has a plan for your life, to give you a future and a hope. The enemy also has a plan, but his leads to death and destruction. Can you identify both God's plan and the enemy's? We encourage you to ask God to show you His wonderful plan. "How precious are your thoughts about me, O God. They cannot be numbered!" (Psalm 139:17-18 NLT).

Write down His thoughts and purposes for you. Also, ask God to show you how the enemy seeks to destroy you. Be alert and fight but also know that "nothing can ever separate us from God's love. Neither death nor life, neither angels nor demons, neither our fears for today nor our worries about tomorrow—not even the powers of hell can separate us from God's love. No power in the sky above or in the earth below—indeed, nothing in all creation will ever be able to separate us from the love of God that is revealed in Christ Jesus our Lord" (Romans 8:38-39).

> **REFLECTION**
> *Explain the difference between God's plan and the enemy's plan.*

DAY 7: Not All Thoughts Are Our Own

Daniel, a young man sixteen years old, had come under an onslaught from the enemy. He couldn't sleep or concentrate. He battled thoughts that he knew were ungodly and was tormented by these thoughts, horrified that he could think them. As a result, he believed he was a horrible person, cut off from all of God's love and goodness.

His parents were extremely concerned, worried that Daniel was spiraling into mental illness. The turning point in the battle for Daniel's mind happened when he discussed his thoughts with a wise minister. The minister showed Daniel 2 Corinthians 10:3-5, "For though we live in the world, we do not wage war as the world does. The weapon we fight with are no the weapons of the world. On the contrary, they have divine power to demolish strongholds. We demolish arguments and every pretension that sets itself up against the knowledge of God, and we take captive every thought to make it obedient to Christ."

In this passage, Paul is speaking of a spiritual war. Central to this war are our thoughts. The "arguments and pretensions" Paul seeks to demolish are thoughts and beliefs that are in direct opposition to the knowledge of God. These thoughts bring an assault of arguments and accusations against God and those created in His image: you and me.

Paul also warns us of a spiritual battle against spiritual forces of evil. In Ephesians 6:10-18, we are charged to "Put on the full armor of God, so that you can take your stand against the devil's schemes." Paul describes these attacks as "flaming arrows." One of the schemes of the devil is to attack us with thoughts.

Kris Vallotten in his book *Spirit Wars* writes, "Because these thoughts are actually manifestations of evil spirits and not just bad ideas, they are compelling—in other words, there is unction to do the act we are contemplating, even though these ideas are contrary to our new nature [in Christ]. Then these same spirits accuse us of originating these thoughts and impulses. If we believe their accusations, we lose confidence in our identity and digress into emotions like depression, anxiety and self-hatred."[1]

Every thought that comes into our mind is not necessarily ours. Daniel was tormented by his thoughts because he believed they originated with him. He believed they represented what he desired. However, Satan had launched a coordinated attack against Daniel. The evil things he heard classmates talking about while standing in line in the cafeteria were compounded by words and images Daniel saw in a history book. Satan was attempting to set up a stronghold in Daniel's life to imprison him.

> Every thought that comes into our mind is not necessarily ours.

The minister taught Daniel that those thoughts were not his own but were an attack of the enemy. The minister prayed with Daniel and took those thoughts captive. When Daniel was freed from the lie that these evil thoughts were his and therefore he was evil, he could run to God instead of feeling as if he was separated from God and His love.

Jesus was also tempted by the devil with thoughts while in the wilderness, but He overcame. We can run to Jesus when we are tempted because Hebrews 4:15-16 says, "For we do not have a high priest who is unable to sympathize with our weaknesses, but we have one who has been tempted in every way, just as we are—yet without sin. Let us then approach the throne of grace with confidence, so that we may receive mercy and find grace to help us in our time of need."

REFLECTION
Where can we go when we are weak from attacks in our thoughts?

Finding Freedom

CHAPTER 6

Healing the Broken Heart

DAY 1: I Saw You

After accidently cutting my finger, I (Tracie) held it over the sink and watched the blood drip out. Something deep inside me groaned in pain: "I really am all alone. No one will be there for me when I am in need."

"Where did that strange thought come from?" I asked myself. God whispered to my heart, "You know." Then I remembered. We had recently moved to a new city where I gave birth to our daughter, Elisa. It had been a difficult delivery. Shortly after she was born, I was taken to the operating room for surgery because I was bleeding.

> When we experience pain, trauma, or loss, the enemy seeks to gain a foothold.

That night, after my husband and family visited and held Elisa and celebrated this precious life, I lay alone in my hospital room. It was then that I noticed that my hands were stained with blood. I felt cold and realized that I was only covered with a thin blanket. None of the nurses had thought to clean me up, get me into a nightgown or give me fresh blankets after my surgery.

A hospital gown lay on a chair across the room. Weak and in pain I reached out and pulled a nightgown from my bag and somehow got it over my head and the IV through the armholes.

Thirteen years later, the trauma of that experience broke the surface of my memory. Those feelings erupted like a geyser. My pain led me to conclude that I was truly alone in this world, and I recognized that I had been living out of that lie for many years.

When we experience something painful or traumatic, we often come to false conclusions about what we have experienced. When we are most vulnerable spiritually, physically and emotionally, the enemy whispers his venom into that pain: lies and accusations against us, against others and against God take root deep in our hearts. These agreements feel so true, because the experience and the pain attached to them are so strong and seem to validate them.

Paul writes in Ephesians 4:26, "In your anger do not sin: Do not let the sun go down while you are still angry, and do not give the devil a foothold."

Anger is most often rooted in pain. I believe that when we experience pain, trauma, or loss, the enemy seeks to gain a foothold. Strongholds are built on footholds.

God ministered to me through a passage of Scripture in Ezekiel 16:4-10, "On the day that you were born your cord was not cut, nor were you washed with water to make you clean, nor were you rubbed with salt or wrapped in cloths. No one looked on you with pity or had compassion enough to do

REFLECTION
Can you remember a time of pain, trauma or loss in which you made an agreement with the enemy?

any of these things for you. Rather, you were thrown out into the open field, for on that day you were born you were despised. Then I passed by and saw you kicking about in your blood, and as you lay there I said to you, "Live!" ... I bathed you with water and washed the blood from you and put ointments on you. I clothed you ... "

God spoke to me that He saw me that day. My pain had not gone unnoticed by Him. He washed my heart with His love and with the water of His Word and replaced that lie with His truth, "I will never leave you or abandon you" (Hebrews 13:5 CEB).

Sunburn

About ten years ago, Craig's extended family vacationed together in South Carolina. By day three, every one of us were sunburned and in pain. Cries of "Don't touch me!" resounded from all. My brother-in-law Brad was the worst. Whenever anyone got within fifteen feet of him, he cringed and yelped in anticipation of possible pain even though no one was near enough to touch him!

Sunburn pain is minor compared to a broken heart. We often react in similar ways to protect ourselves from further emotional pain. In numerous scriptures, the Bible speaks of a broken heart: "The Lord is close to the brokenhearted and saves those who are crushed in spirit" (Psalm 34:18). "He heals the brokenhearted and binds up their wounds" (Psalm 147:3). David said, "My heart is wounded within me" (Psalm 109:22). Wounds of the heart cut the deepest of all injuries.

Even though it has no bones, the heart can be broken. As a result of these wounds, our hearts are raw. We live in fear of the next blow, and in that rawness, our emotions sometimes betray us. We react out of our wound. James 4:1, "What causes fights and quarrels among you? Don't they come from your desires that battle within you?" Most of our interpersonal conflicts are the result of our reacting out of pain within our hearts.

> Most of our interpersonal conflicts are the result of our reacting out of pain within our hearts.

As a young boy, Henry experienced deep rejection when his father abandoned his family. As a grown man in his fifties, Henry's heart was still raw and unhealed. He lived in fear of being rejected. He reacted out of the hurt of an eight-year-old boy rejected by his father whenever he perceived rejection from people in his life. Henry was sabotaging his relationships and medicating his pain through alcohol, drugs and self-destructive behavior.

God promises to bind up the brokenhearted (Isaiah 61:1). He knows our pain and every tear we cry (Psalm 56:8). He longs to heal us, and it is though His wounds that we are healed (Isaiah 53:5). Healing is offered to us, but we need to choose it.

"Who among you fears the Lord and obeys the word

of his servant? Let him who walks in the dark, who has no light, trust in the name of the Lord and rely on his God. But now, all you who light fires and provide yourselves with flaming torches, go, walk in the light of your fires and of the torches you have set ablaze" (Isaiah 50:10-11).

When we live out of the pain of our hearts, we are living in darkness. We don't perceive things clearly. The unhealed heart is "deceitful above all else" (Jeremiah 17:9). God offers us His light and His healing, but we often choose to employ our own ways of protecting ourselves and comforting ourselves. God beckons us to put our faith in Him, because "everything that does not come from faith is sin" (Romans 14:23).

Henry chose God's comfort and chose to come out of the darkness of his pain and into the light of God's love. As God began to heal Henry's heart, he was free to live free from rejection and addiction and free to walk in healthy relationships with others.

REFLECTION
Can you identify the wounds of your heart and your reaction to them?

Listen to your heart's thoughts, emotions and reactions. They may reveal the story of your wounded heart. The road to the healing of the heart leads through acknowledging our pain to God, forgiving those who have hurt us, repenting of the lies we have believed and for the ways we have gone outside of God's will to protect and comfort ourselves, asking forgiveness for hurting others and allowing God to heal us.

DAY 3

Put Away Childish Things

Most counselors and psychologists agree that many issues with which we struggle are rooted in our childhoods. This is because young children are like sponges and take in everything, good and bad, to form convictions about the world around them, the people around them and even opinions about God. The convictions children form are like impressions in wet concrete that, when hardened, serves as a foundation for their lives.

Because children are so powerless and vulnerable, they lack the ability to deal with victimization and other traumatic experiences. This is why many people who are abused believe that they deserved it or that they are bad. Because we all try to make sense of what is happening around us and to us, our conclusions become beliefs that often dictate unhealthy patterns of behavior for years to come.

> Janey was in her fifties when she allowed Jesus to heal her shame and pain.

We see Jesus' heart toward children when He says in Matthew 18:6-7, "If anyone causes one of these little ones who believe in me to stumble, it would be better for them to have a large millstone hung around their neck and to be drowned in the depths of the sea. Woe to the world because of the things that cause people to stumble! Such things must come, but woe to the person through whom they come!"

The Greek word for "things that cause people to stumble" is *skandalon*[1], meaning to entrap or entice to sin.[2]

When Janey was a young girl walking home one night, some boys surrounded her and pushed her against a wall. Feeling terrified and ashamed, she pushed the memory down deep, trying to deny that it ever happened. This became a pattern in her life: Whenever she encountered something painful, she emotionally shut down. She refused to deal with things, often lying or justifying her behavior to protect herself. Her actions caused great pain in her relationships. When we live a life of denial, we hide ourselves from God as well as others, and shut ourselves off from God ministering healing in our lives.

1 Corinthians 13:11 (NKJV) says, "When I was a child, I spoke as a child, I understood as a child, I thought as a child; but when I became a man, I put away childish things."

David A. Seamands, in his book, *Redeeming the Past*, explains that "childish things" speaks to a combination of emotional and spiritual immaturity. He claims that unhealed painful memories from childhood can cause people to be stuck "at a certain age and stage of development" emotionally. Paul says he "put away childish things," which Seamands defines as "to render inoperative, inactive, or powerless; to free from that which has been keeping one bound."[2]

> **REFLECTION**
> *Can you think of any pain from your childhood that has caused patterns of sin or unhealthy behaviors in your life?*

We can be entrapped and bound by the beliefs and patterns of sin in our lives as a result of traumatic things we experienced as a child. Janey was in her fifties when she allowed Jesus to heal her shame and pain. She faced her pain, forgave those who had hurt her and put away her childish ways of shutting down and protecting herself whenever she felt afraid and insecure. Now she has been walking in freedom for twenty years and is helping others get set free!

Shame

"Who does Linda look like?" we asked her parents. Linda and her mom and dad exchanged glances before her father answered, "She looks like herself." We were all enjoying dinner together and the conversation quickly moved on to other topics. Linda and her husband had been married for several years and had two beautiful children. About a year later, Linda shared her testimony of how God had healed her and set her free. When Craig and I read it, we were astonished. In her testimony Linda disclosed that she had been adopted and how God set her free from rejection and the anger she had felt toward her birth mother.

> We believe we will be rejected if others see us for who we truly are.

Previously Linda had never told anyone that she had been adopted—neither her husband nor anyone else outside of her family. When we asked her why she had kept this secret, she told us that she was afraid that her husband would view her and her parents differently. She didn't want anyone to know that she was adopted because she felt shame.

Christine Cain describes what shame is and what it does: "Shame makes us feel small. Flawed. Not good enough. And controlled. Shame is the fear of being unworthy, and it adversely affects our relationship with God, ourselves, and others. It greatly hinders our ability to receive God's unconditional love—and share it with others."[3]

Guilt is feeling bad about the things we have done. Guilt can be healthy when it leads us to seek and receive God's forgiveness. Shame is how we feel about ourselves because of our actions or what has been done to us by others. Shame defines us as worthless, and tells us that something is inherently wrong with us. Shame keeps us from seeking and receiving God's love, healing and forgiveness because we believe that we do not deserve His grace and mercy. We hide ourselves from God and the people around us, just as Adam and Eve did. "O my God, I am too ashamed to lift up my face to you" (Ezra 9:6). "I live in disgrace all day long, and my face is covered with shame" (Psalm 44:15). We obscure our true selves, because we believe we will be rejected if others see us for who we truly are. We live our lives hidden in the dark.

> **REFLECTION**
> *Are you hiding? Can you identify how your shame affects your relationship with God and with others?*

The Bible tells us in 1 John 1:7 (NLT), "But if we are living in the light, as God is in the light, then we have fellowship with each other, and the blood of Jesus, his Son, cleanses us from all sin."

Hiding in the darkness, keeps us from intimacy with God and with the people in our lives. In 1 John 1:9, we are promised that if we confess our sins to God he will forgive us and cleanse us from all sins. James 5:16 says, "confess your sins to each other and pray for each other so that you may be healed."

When we come out of hiding and into the light that exposes our true selves, the miracle of healing happens. When Linda brought the truth of her adoption into the light, she also experienced God's unconditional love and acceptance from her husband and from those around her. She was set free from shame!

Waves of Grief and Waves of Grace

In November 1995, Craig, I and our two little boys were on a short-term mission trip to Guatemala and El Salvador. I (Tracie) miscarried while on this trip. It was early in my pregnancy, but our hearts had already embraced this new life and all the promise with it. Craig and I were devastated.

The day I began to miscarry, we were visiting the beach in El Salvador. Later, the Lord used my memories of the beach and the ocean as He spoke into my bruised heart. God showed me that grief comes in like waves, but He promised me that each wave of grief would be followed by a wave of grace, just like the waves of the ocean keep coming one right after another. He was faithful to that promise. After every wave of grief, a wave of grace that matched the previous wave perfectly washed over me, every single time.

> I learned to anticipate the waves of grace and comfort that always faithfully came.

1 Peter 4:10 exhorts us to "faithfully administer the manifold grace of God." Picture a diamond prism: As light is refracted through the prism, it bursts into every color of the rainbow. That is the manifold grace of God. The same word *manifold* is used in 1 Peter 1:6-7, where we are encouraged to rejoice even while suffering "all kinds of trials," promising us that through them our faith will be refined and proved genuine like pure gold. There is manifold grace for the manifold trials of life. There is a color of grace that corresponds exactly to the color of the trial we are going through.

John 1:16 (NASB) tells us, "For of His fullness we have all received, and grace upon grace." Just as waves upon waves upon waves crash onto the shore, so do grace upon grace upon grace crest upon our lives. I am reminded of the scripture, "Deep calls to deep in the roar of your waterfalls; all your waves and breakers have swept over me" (Psalm 42:7).

Immediately after my miscarriage, grief came like tsunami waves that dragged me under. Over time, the waves lessened in strength and frequency and only knocked me down momentarily, finally receding to waves that lapped at my feet. I learned to anticipate the waves of grace and comfort that always faithfully came, that still come, even today. I have come to know, to rely upon and to praise "the God and Father of our Lord Jesus Christ, the Father of compassion and of all comfort, who comforts us in all troubles" (2 Corinthians 1:3). He is ever faithful.

> **REFLECTION**
> What does it mean to know that there is a grace for every grief you encounter in life?

About a month after I miscarried, we drove from Oklahoma to Pennsylvania to visit family. We noticed a sign for the Precious Moments Chapel in Joplin, Missouri. On a whim, we decided to visit. This was a tourist destination, with a gift shop selling numerous items related to the popular collectible Precious Moments figurines. The artist, Samuel J. Butcher, had also built a chapel on the site. At the front of the chapel, the artist painted Jesus with His hands outstretched and surrounded by angels welcoming people into heaven. One angel is depicted as taking away someone's crutches and another angel as giving a baby to a couple as they entered into the gates of heaven. Oh, how that scene ministered to me. What a beautiful color of grace!

DAY 6: You Don't Have Anything to Prove

Earlier I (Tracie) shared about my midnight encounter with the mountain deity, Paccha Mama in Cusco, Peru. About a week later, I had another encounter awaken me out of my restless sleep. This encounter resulted from an event that had happened a few days before when Craig and I had toured Lago Titicaca, a beautiful lake high in the Andes Mountains. To get there, we had to take a six-hour overnight bus trip. When we arrived, I found that my camera had been stolen with hundreds of pictures in it capturing our time in Peru.

> His words reached deep within my heart, restoring and making me whole.

The loss of my camera and photos stirred up feelings of bereavement comparable to those that I had felt when we lived in Peru twenty years earlier. We had moved to Peru, planning to live and minister there for three years, but unexpectantly we had to return within six months to the U.S. The death of that vision for our ministry in Peru was a devastating loss to us.

Again, in the middle of the night, tossing and turning, suspended somewhere between sleep and awake, I was pouring out my heart to God. I told Him that I wanted to be brave and strong, and do great things for Him. I wanted to go wherever He wanted me to go and do whatever He asked me to do. But I was not capable. I was not strong enough. He should know that I did not have what it took—neither now nor twenty years earlier. God should take all those dreams and purposes He had given me and give them to someone else, someone who remained strong, confident in His care no matter what happened.

God spoke to me that night. He spoke deep into my heart, deep into the layers of disappointment, loss and the pain that were twenty years in the making. "You don't have anything to prove," He said. With tears streaming down my face, I sat up in bed. His words reached deep within my heart, restoring and making me whole.

Two weeks later, Craig and I hiked the Inca Trail. We were part of a group that included a young man from the Netherlands, a young couple from Belgium, and a couple in their sixties from Russia. The young Europeans, in their twenties, led our team far in front of me with incredible speed, and the Russian couple never seemed to tire. The team often waited for me as I lagged behind. For the entire four days, I felt sick and weak as I battled altitude sickness. Craig was gracious to stay back with me and patiently waited, encouraging me to stop and catch my breath as necessary; but I was frustrated and ashamed of my weakness.

REFLECTION
Can you identify anything that you are trying to prove to God, to others?

The highest point of the trail reached almost 14,000 feet in altitude and had been named "Dead Woman's Pass." The irony of that name did not escape me. God's words, "You don't have anything to prove," kept me going, assuring me that I was going to make it, even if I was the weakest and slowest member of my team.

Cheered on by one hundred of my fellow hikers and despite my weakness, my reward was reaching the Sun Gate. Together we sat silently watching in awe as the lost city of Macchu Picchu appeared to rise up through the dissipating cloud layer below us.

Knowing that I don't have anything to prove doesn't result in me doing less, but empowers me to do things I could never do in my own strength. Not having to prove anything to God or anyone else frees me to do many things that I never believed I could do.

Sadly, many of us live much of our lives trying to prove our worth to God, to others and even to ourselves. Paul, however, boasted in his weaknesses. He wrote in 2 Corinthians 12:9-10, "My grace is sufficient for you, for my power is made perfect in weakness. Therefore, I will boast all the more gladly about my weaknesses, so that Christ's power may rest on me. That is why, for Christ's sake, I delight in weaknesses.... For when I am weak, then I am strong."

Have You Been Dropped, Burned or Crippled?

Mephibosheth was a young man who lived the first part of his life believing a lie. He hid out in the town of Lo Debar, believing his life was in great danger. Since his grandfather,

Saul, was no longer the king of Israel, Mephibosheth was told it was only a matter of time until David, the new king, found him. He had been told the stories about kings who throughout the generations destroyed all family members of the former king, even decapitated them.

Mephibosheth lived not only in emotional pain but also physical pain. As a small child, he was crippled when a servant girl dropped him as they were fleeing from the new king advancing toward the palace. Mephibosheth was emotionally and physically scarred, and like the stones of the fallen wall around Jerusalem, he appeared "burned"—unable to fulfill his destiny.

> God is calling forth His people who have been burned and broken.

One dreaded day, the new king's servants arrived in Lo Debar to find the grandson of King Saul. When they brought him to the palace, Mephibosheth fell on his face in terror and prostrated himself before the king. Mephibosheth couldn't believe his ears when he heard the king say, "Do not fear, for I will surely show you kindness for Jonathan your father's sake, and will restore to you all the land of Saul your grandfather; and you shall eat bread at my table continually" (2 Samuel 9:7).

Unknown to Mephibosheth, David had made a covenant with Mephibosheth's father Jonathan years before. They had pledged to take care of each other's families if anything ever happened to them. When Jonathan was killed in battle with his father Saul, David remembered his covenant with his best friend Jonathan. He was committed to keeping his promise.

For years, Mephibosheth had believed a lie. He was convinced that David would kill him, but all the while David was pursuing him and had his best interests at heart. Mephibosheth was esteemed by David and given the honor of sitting at the king's table. Every need Mephibosheth had was completely met.

Have you been "burned or dropped?" Like Mephibosheth, did you ever feel as if someone "dropped" you, crippling you for life? We meet so many people with a clear call of God on their lives, but who feel as if they have been burned emotionally or dropped by someone they trusted. Some were burned by a relationship deteriorating after spending a lot of time developing it. In other cases, they became disillusioned when a natural father or mother or a spiritual father or mother disappointed them. They gave up and live in deep disappointment and fear that the Lord will never be able to use them again.

We live in a fallen world, but we were raised with Christ when we were redeemed, bought back by the blood Jesus shed on the cross two thousand years ago. Jesus came to give us abundant life and set us free (John 8:32). Step by step, we reclaim what Satan has stolen from us—in our homes, in our workplaces, at school—as believers, we have the privilege of pointing the way home to those who are lost. God has a loving plan of redemption for every believer and seeks to accomplish His plan through ordinary people like us.

In these days, God is calling forth His people who have been burned and broken. God is healing them and giving them a job to do. When a metal such as iron is heated in the fire, it is refined and tempered, and it gains great strength. Those who have faced difficulties and allowed God to temper them are refined and ready to be used because they are stronger. For example, couples who are victorious after experiencing marital struggles are the ones to help other couples who are struggling in their marriages.

> **REFLECTION**
> *What is the lie Mephibosheth lived under? How did he find freedom?*

Find your place on God's wall of service by helping others find freedom. God loves to use burned stones who have felt dropped or crippled! If this is you, receive the grace of God today from your heavenly Father to be made whole through His son Jesus Christ. God wants to bless you, make you strong and give you a great inheritance. You will be stronger!

Finding Freedom

CHAPTER 7

Receiving the Father Heart of God

DAY 1

Homecoming

"But while he was still a long way off, his father saw him and was filled with compassion for him; he ran to his son, threw his arms around him and kissed him" (Luke 15:20).

I (Tracie) met and prayed with Annie several times during the past several years. She had fallen into sin, which entrapped her into a vicious pattern of self-destructive behavior. One time, Annie told me that she had repented of her self-destructive pattern of sin and was walking in a degree of freedom. She believed God had forgiven her, but she could not feel God. She felt detached and far away from him.

> Feel His joy and celebration and His delight in you.

The Holy Spirit prompted me to say, "You need to experience your homecoming!" When the prodigal son returned home to his father, he experienced his father's joy and celebration at his return. He was reunited with his father and their relationship was restored. Annie replied with great pain, "Oh no, I can't face Father God."

"But what if Jesus brought you to Father God? What if He started the conversation and spoke for you?" I asked. Annie answered immediately, "Oh yes, I could go to the Father with Jesus at my side and with Him going before me."

Together we prayed for Annie to experience her homecoming and reunion with her Heavenly Father. As we finished praying, Annie smiled with relief and joy.

In Luke 15:11-32, Jesus told the story of the Prodigal Son because He wants us to know the heart of God the Father, our Father. He is not harsh, demanding and unforgiving. Jesus said, "I am the "way" to the Father" (John 14:6). He tells us, "if you've seen me you've seen the Father" (John 14:9). He wants us to know our Father God. He is the mediator for us (1 Timothy 2:5). Jesus leads us and presents us to the Father who has always loved us and who is waiting for us with open arms.

REFLECTION
What would it be like if you truly believed that God's arms were open wide to you and His delight was in you?

We encourage you to read the story of the Prodigal Son. Put yourself in this story and see the Father's eyes searching for you and His arms wide open. Feel His joy and celebration and His delight in you. Hear Him say to you, "Welcome Home!"

Dealing with Father Issues

DAY 2

During a television interview, Olympic gold medalist Michael Phelps shared how he had been confronted with the need to deal with his father issues.[1] After being arrested for drunk driving in 2014, Phelps realized this was his cry for help from his deep-rooted feelings of abandonment from his father. At age 9, Phelps had watched his mother and father go through a divorce. This led to resentment growing in his heart and avoidance of his father.

During Phelps' substance abuse treatment, breakthrough began to happen. When his father visited him, Phelps opened up and healing began to take place between them. Phelps said in the interview, "I used to think of myself as a swimmer and nobody else." Those are sad words, but, like Phelps, many people feel as if their worth is dependent only upon achievement. Because of the lack of relationship with their father or mother, many people suffer from a love deficit that also affects their ability to give and receive love from others. Michael shared how he often pushed people out of his life because his broken relationship with his dad early on taught him to build walls in his heart. So it is with many of us.

> Many people feel as if their worth is dependent only upon achievement.

During my growing-up years, my dad often worked two jobs to support our family. I (Craig) loved and respected my dad. I knew that he loved me and was proud of me, but I didn't have the relationship with him that I really longed for. As a sensitive kid, I didn't have the affirmation that I really needed. As a result, I often felt as if I had to prove myself. I struggled with feelings of insecurity, and this bled over into my relationship with God. Seeing God as my Father was difficult because I didn't feel close to my earthly dad at that time. I knew Jesus as my Savior and Lord, and I loved God, but something was missing.

All this changed one evening in college during a worship service. As we were worshiping, I experienced what I call "liquid love" being poured all over me. I heard the Father saying, "I love you, son." At that moment, this insecure, fearful teenager began to dance like David danced and I began to shout like Joshua bringing down the mighty walls of Jericho—I haven't stopped since that night.

Romans 8:15 says, "For you did not receive the spirit of bondage again to fear, but you received the Spirit of adoption by whom we cry out, 'Abba, Father.'" That word "Abba" is the most affectionate term a Jewish child can call his father—it literally means "Daddy." You and I do not have to live in bondage to the fear of rejection, pushing people out of our lives because we are afraid of being hurt, building walls because it's difficult to trust others. We have a Father who wants to heal our "father issues." He is Abba. We can open our hearts and trust Him today.

REFLECTION
How does Father God want to minister to your heart cry for love?

Freedom from The Orphan Spirit

Dave came into my (Craig's) office. He said that he was struggling because he did not feel connected in our church. After hearing his complaints, I probed deeper into his history of bouncing from church to church and of never feeling connected anywhere. I learned that Dave had been orphaned by his parents when he was young. As a result, he had learned some unhealthy independent tendencies from living under a cloud of rejection. I tenderly affirmed the Father's love for Dave and our love for him as a church, and carefully asked him if he would be willing for me to pray with him to be healed and set free from this orphan spirit. Immediately his defenses went up. He stormed out of my office. That was the last conversation he allowed me to have with him.

Dave's story reminds me of Maria, who was also orphaned as a little girl. But she is a vibrant part of our church family and is one of the most loving individuals that I have ever met. Not a trace of abandonment or rejection is reflected in the way that she gives and receives love.

> They love God but do not know the love of God.

Zach was a young man raised by both his parents, but in a home broken from alcohol and drug abuse as well as constant physical and verbal abuse. Newly saved, Zach came to our church, seeking healing in his life and freedom from his past. I remember a small group of us ministering to him and sharing Psalm 27:10, "When my father and my mother forsake me, then the Lord will take care of me."

With tears of joy streaming down his face, Zach shared that he never felt so much love and had thought it impossible to feel so much a part of a family.

What is the difference between Dave, Maria and Zach? They all struggled with profound feelings of abandonment and neglect, but Maria and Zach received the Father's healing, forgave those who hurt them and broke agreement with the lies of the enemy that defined them before in their rejection. They are now defined as children of God placed into His family. They allowed God to be a Father to the fatherless and to set them into a family (Psalm 68:5).

My heart breaks for the "Daves" of this world. They love God but do not know the love of God. They are saved but they are still broken. They go to church services, but they never feel connected. This orphan spirit is real and it will cause us to believe that no one, including God, could ever love us or can be trusted.

This orphan spirit will manifest in many ways and hinder us from love. Those who carry an orphan spirit live under the belief that they never fit, that they are constantly on the outside looking in. They believe they will always be rejected, so they often reject others first before they can be rejected. They often feel a sense of unworthiness, insecurity, defensiveness and loneliness. Because those with orphan spirits do not feel as if they are good enough, they will either be driven to perform to be loved or they will give in to destructive behaviors because they don't think it's even worth trying.

> **REFLECTION**
> *Am I willing to forgive others who have rejected me, open my heart to the Father's love, and to be loved by a church family?*

Just as Maria and Zach made decisions to allow their Heavenly Father to define them and not their earthly father (or leader or teacher or anyone else who rejected them), you too can open your heart to the Father's love and declare, "I am accepted in the Beloved" (Ephesians 1:6).

Daddy's Delight

One of Jill's most vivid memories of her childhood is when she and her cousins were playing outside, running around the house. Her father called saying it was time to go. Caught up in the fun, she continued to run with the other children. The next time she came around to the front of the house, her dad gave her a swift, hard kick.

Jill was four years old. This experience taught Jill that her father was a hard man, a harsh disciplinarian. She did not feel safe, accepted and loved by her father. Rather, she feared him and sought to please him to escape punishment.

> How we see God as Father is strongly influenced by our experiences with our earthly fathers.

When Danielle thinks of her dad, it brings up feelings of betrayal, pain and anger at her memories of his sexual abuse. Danielle could relate to God as Jesus and as the Holy Spirit, but she was unable to see God as her loving Father. Her pain was like cataracts on the eyes of her heart.

In more than 165 times in the Gospels, Jesus spoke of

God as our Father. Jesus was intent on introducing mankind to His Father who is also our Father. In John 14:7, He promised us, "If you really know me, you will know my Father as well. From now on, you do know him and have seen him." And after His resurrection, He proclaimed that His Father was now our Father (John 20:17).

The theme of Father God continues throughout the New Testament. Through the Scriptures we are invited to know God as our Father.

In Psalms 17:8, God refers to us as the "apple of His eye." In Spanish it reads, "la niña de Sus ojos," which literally means, "the little girl of His eyes," or you could say, "Daddy's delight."

No earthly father is perfect, so relating to God as Father often stirs up a whole gamut of emotions within each of us. How we see God as Father is strongly influenced by our experiences with our earthly fathers and mothers, as well as authority figures in our lives. To find freedom to embrace God as our Father, we need to do the following:

REFLECTION
How does God want to reveal Himself to you?

- Sort through our experiences with our fathers, mothers, and authority figures in our lives. Identify those experiences as either, "like Father God" and "not like Father God."
- Thank God for the ways our fathers were like God and forgive them for the ways that were not like God.

- Repent of any ways we have continued the same hurtful actions of our fathers.
- Receive God's healing for how we have been rejected, abandoned, neglected, hurt or abused.
- Ask God to show us who He really is, allow Him to reveal Himself to us as our Father.

"How great is the love the Father has lavished on us, that we should be called children of God! And that is what we are!" (1 John 3:1).

Don't Give Way to Fear

I (Tracie) find the Old Testament character Sarah fascinating. When God's promise of a child delays, she takes things into her own hands and compels Abraham into bringing forth the child Ishmael through Hagar. God, in His timing, is faithful to His promise as Sarah ultimately gives birth to Isaac. Family drama ensues when Sarah banishes Hagar and Ishmael into the wilderness.

Despite Sarah's problematic behavior, Peter mentions her with honor and exhorts women to emulate her in 1 Peter 3:6: "You are her daughters if you do what is right and do not give way to fear."

Hebrews 11:8-9 tells us that Abraham by faith obeyed and left his homeland even though he didn't know where he was going and "made his home in the promised land like a stranger in a foreign country" living in tents. Abraham comes home one day, tells Sarah they are moving. "Where?" she asks. "I have no idea," he answers.

They move from the only place they know and from all the people they know. As they enter Egypt, Abraham tells Sarah, "I know what a beautiful woman you are. When the Egyptians see you they will say, 'This is his wife.' Then they will kill me but will let you live. Say you are my sister, so that I will be treated well for your sake and my life will be spared because of you."

Sarah ends up in Pharaoh's palace to be taken as his wife. God inflicts "serious" diseases on Pharaoh leading him to give her back to Abraham (Genesis 12:10-20). Then again, Abraham pulls the sister thing as they are about to enter kingdom of Gerar, which results in the king taking her as his wife. This time God intervenes by giving the king a warning through a dream that he is a dead man (Genesis 20:1-18). The king promptly returns her to Abraham.

> All of us experience consequences as a result of other people's actions.

Imagine what it must have been like for Sarah waiting in the Pharaoh's bedchamber and then again in the king's. She had no rights. Her life was completely out of her control. Twice, Abraham has put her life into the hands of strangers in order to save his own.

All of us experience consequences as a result of other people's actions. Actions that left us wounded or compromised our wellbeing. We are passed over for that promotion, fired for no reason, victimized by someone who had power when we did not, left alone to suffer. If we are really honest, we have very little control over anything.

Fear causes us to reach out to gain control. Fear drove Sarah to give Hagar to Abraham and then again to banish Hagar and Ishmael. Fear drives us to go outside of God's plans and His ways. It drives us to sin.

1 John 4:18 says, "There is no fear in love. But perfect love drives out fear." For God did not give us a spirit of timidity [fear], but of power, of love, and of self-discipline [self-control]" (2 Timothy 1:7).

REFLECTION
What fear(s) do you live with?

We can choose to do what is right. We can choose to trust God and not give way to fear. "Submit yourselves, then, to God. Resist the devil, and he will flee from you" James 4:7. When we give up control to God, trusting in His love and goodness, He will deliver us, just as He did Sarah time and time again.

Healing of our Memories and Emotions

DAY 6

Our Father God loves us more than we can ever comprehend, and He desires for us to be healed in every area of our lives. This includes being healed of painful memories and receiving healing in our emotions.

Sometimes the term "healing of memories" is used to explain emotional healing. To receive healing of memories means to be healed of lie-filled memories or to have our broken hearts healed. Sometimes our present emotional pain comes from the misinterpretations (lies) embedded in our memories and not from the memories themselves. For example, an incest victim feels shame not only because she was molested but also because she believes the lie that it was her fault instead of the perpetuator's. When the lie is exposed, the victim can receive healing of memories that leads to freedom.

> Although we remember what happened, the pain associated with the memory has been healed through Jesus.

Some of us may have painful memories from our relationship with our parents. God desires for us to be whole and wants to minister his healing to those memories. Psalm 27:10 (NLT) says, "Even if my father and mother abandon me, the Lord will hold me close [take care of me]."

A young man and his fiancée came to LaVerne and me (Larry) for premarital counseling. The young man had experienced many hurts in his life. His father constantly blamed him for the problems because the son had been conceived out of wedlock. The young man was hurting and needed healing. I asked him if he was willing to forgive his dad. He was willing. We laid our hands on him and prayed for him to be healed of the painful memories that he had experienced while growing up.

A few months later, the young man had a wonderful wedding. His father was at his wedding, but there was no longer a wall between them. The pain was gone. God supernaturally healed the young man because Jesus Christ took that pain on the cross two thousand years ago.

The healing of our memories does not mean that we no longer recall what has happened. Although we remember what happened, the pain associated with the memory has been healed through Jesus. We can look back and give praise to God for His healing on our lives and His grace and strength to go on.

An important scriptural key to being healed and set free is in Matthew 6:14-15: "For if you forgive men when they sin against you, your heavenly Father will also forgive you. But if you do not forgive men their sins, your Father will not forgive your sins."

REFLECTION
What can hinder us from being healed of painful memories?

This is important! We must forgive those who have hurt us to receive what Father God has for us.

DAY 7: From Slavery to Sonship

"Even so we, when we were children, were in bondage under the elements of the world. But when the fullness of the time had come, God sent forth His Son, born of a woman, born under the law, to redeem those who were under the law, that we might receive the adoption as sons.

And because you are sons, God has sent forth the Spirit of His Son into your hearts, crying out, "Abba, Father!" Therefore you are no longer a slave but a son, and if a son, then an heir of God through Christ" (Galatians 4:3-7).

As followers of Jesus, many of us continue to live as if we are imprisoned by sin and our past. Because of Jesus, the prison doors have been opened wide, but we choose to live behind bars of bondages of shame, guilt, and condemnation. We have good news for you: Jesus not only opened the prison doors, He has come to set the captives free (Isaiah 61:1). You are no longer a slave to fear, to sin, or to your past. You are a son and daughter of God!

> You are no longer a slave to fear, to sin, or to your past.

A young man shared with me (Craig) his constant struggle with self-doubt, insecurity, and condemnation. He was raised in what I perceived a stable and healthy Christian home, yet he had a really hard time seeing God as Father and having a close, intimate relationship with God. I asked him to share with me about his prayer life. He confessed that his prayer life was at best sporadic, and when he did pray, it was more of a laundry list of confessing his sins or asking for his needs to be met. It was not a Father-son relationship. It was more of a striving than a resting.

We decided to meet together to begin a journey, moving from slavery into sonship. As we looked at God's Word (as listed below), and the truth of how God really saw him, he was set free to have the relationship with God he always longed for. This is the same relationship the Father longs to have with you as a "son or daughter whom he loves" (Matthew 3:17 CEB).

REFLECTION
In what ways do you still live behind the prison doors of sin and your past?

Slavery	**Sonship**
Beg	Possess (Luke 12:29-32)
Petition	Declare (Psalm 103:1-5)
Poverty	Abundant supply (Philippians 4:19)
Works of the law	Walk of faith (Galatians 3:5)
Undeserving/ unworthy	Heirs of God because Christ is worthy (Galatians 4:7)
Trying to prove yourself	Living from the Father's approval (Matthew 3:17)
Rejection/ self-hatred	Accepted in the Beloved (Ephesians 1:3)
Punishment	Discipline (Hebrews 12:6-7)
Serves out of fear	Serves out of love (I John 4:18)
Bondage	Freedom (Romans 8:15)
Burden	Call (Matthew 11:28-30)
Restriction	Revelation (Ephesians 3:17)
Sees God as Master	Sees God as Father (I John 3:1)
Distant respect	Intimate relationship (Hebrews 10:19-23)

We encourage you to take the time that is needed to prayerfully read through this list and discern how you see yourself. Do you see yourself as a slave or as a son? Begin to take the journey out of slavery into sonship.

CHAPTER 8

Staying Free

DAY 1 — Keep the Doors Shut!

Some time ago, Joe, a married man, came for help because of his struggle with homosexual attraction. I (Craig) will never forget Joe's heart of repentance that day and his desire to honor his wife and to honor the Lord with his sexuality. As Joe repented and broke agreement with any of his past sins and actions in this area, it was so powerful watching the Holy Spirit minister His cleansing power, releasing forgiveness and freedom from all shame. Joe and I met a few more times and he literally was glowing with the new-found freedom in his life.

Months later, Joe returned. His countenance was heavy as he shared that he was really struggling again with a strong pull to go back to a previous homosexual relationship. After talking for a little while, I asked him, "What opened the door to this desire again?" He said that every day he drives by this guy's house on the way to work, and that he has been so close to stopping in to see him. I further inquired if it was possible for him to take a different route to work to avoid all contact with this guy. He said there was, but it was a longer drive. I asked him what he was willing to do to be free?

> Walking in freedom is a partnership with the Holy Spirit!

This is an important question for us all to answer because Jesus paid the price for our freedom, but we must be willing to walk it out. Philippians 2:12 says, "Work out your own salvation with fear and trembling; for it is God who works in you both to will and to work for His good pleasure." Walking in freedom is a partnership with the Holy Spirit!

By driving by that guy's house every day, Joe allowed a door to stay open, which the enemy used to taunt him. After our conversation and prayer for strength, Joe made a decision to shut that door and take another road to work. Today, Joe is flourishing in his relationship with Jesus. God has restored his marriage.

Galatians 5:1 says, "Stand fast therefore in the liberty by which Christ has made us free, and do not be entangled again with a yoke of bondage." I believe so many of us are not able to continue in our freedom because we have allowed doors to stay open in our lives that keep pulling us back to our old way of thinking or our old way of living. There are five doors in Scripture that we need to keep shut and guard. As we do, we will see freedom released in our lives:

REFLECTION
How is the enemy trying to rob you of your freedom in Christ?

Door of our eyes – Psalm 101:3.
Door of our ears – John 10:4-5.
Door of our mind – Philippians 4:6-7.
Door of our mouth – Ephesians 4:29.
Door of our sexuality – 1 Corinthians 6:18-20.

Steps to Freedom

DAY 2

The Lord's freedom from strongholds in our lives can be experienced instantly, but often true and lasting freedom is attained by following a process of steps the Lord gives in His Word. The Scripture tells us in Psalm 37:23, "the steps of a good man are ordered by the Lord." Here are a few biblical steps that help us find freedom:

1. **Faith unlocks the door.** If we hide behind a locked door, attempting to bulletproof ourselves from hurts, we harden our hearts. God wants to expose and free us. How? It's simple. John 8:32 says that when you believe in Christ, you "shall know the truth, and the truth shall make you free." Jesus Christ, who is truth, makes men and women free.

   > If the devil has stolen our peace, our joy, our health, or our hope; today is our day to claim it back from the enemy!

   We become free from being captives to sin such as false notions, hurts, mistakes and prejudices that entangle and enslave the soul. We fall into the arms of Him whose yoke is easy and whose burden is light. We can trust Jesus to restore our lives. As we confess the truth of God's Word, Romans 10:17 says that faith is built. Only then, can we begin to experience God's wholeness.

2. **Stake your claim.** God promised the children of Israel the fertile land of Canaan. It was legally their land because God promised it to them. But they had

to receive it by going in, taking it from their enemies and staking the claim for themselves. The same truth applies to us today. We need to take back the areas of our lives the devil has stolen from us.

If the devil has stolen our peace, our joy, our health, or our hope; today is our day to claim it back from the enemy! Claim back from the devil the specific areas he has stolen from us. When we take Him at His Word, the Lord honors His covenant with us!

3. **Receive prayer from a trusted friend.** For help in your restoration process, you may want to humbly seek the counsel of a godly friend or spiritual father or mother. He or she can assist you on how to obtain God's forgiveness, receive healing in your emotions and gain the strength to sin no more.

4. **Be patient.** Do not expect everything to change overnight. Submit to the timing of the Lord. I (Larry) met a couple in Dallas, Texas, a few years ago that desperately wanted to have children. They tried to have a baby for seventeen years and refused to quit believing. A year later I was in Dallas and saw them holding their baby boy after trusting God for seventeen long years. Regardless of your prior experiences, you need to believe again for total freedom. This means you must allow the Lord to strengthen and season you through the process.

5. **Keep your branches growing over the wall.** God is calling you to be a healthy, believer who lives in

freedom and helps other find freedom. Even if you have not yet experienced complete freedom, the Lord will teach you to help others find freedom as He continues to heal you, if you keep your eyes on Jesus.

"Joseph, a man of moral and spiritual strength, was likened to a young fruit tree with its branches going over the well wall" (Genesis 49:22). The moisture from the well kept the tree watered and bearing fruit. Your branches will grow abundantly over the wall too if you are constantly watered by the Word of God and the Holy Spirit. You will be sure to bear fruit for Him through helping others find freedom.

> **REFLECTION**
> *What are five steps we can take to find freedom?*

Abiding in the Vine

DAY 3

John 15:1-17 records Jesus' teaching of "The Vine and the Branches." In it, Jesus teaches us what it means to live our life in Him. He came that we may "have life, and have it to the full" (John 10:10). Jesus uses a vineyard for His object lesson, in which He is the vine and God the Father is the vinedresser. You and I are the branches.

Jesus' teaching holds several important keys to walking in the freedom He accomplished for us. The word "abide" is used ten times in this passage. Jesus says to "abide in Me." To abide means to dwell and to remain. He conquered sin and death so that you and I could have a relationship with

Him. We abide in Him through relationship with Him and through obedience to His word.

A branch can do nothing by itself. It must be connected to the vine just as we must be connected to the Vine, Jesus. The body of Christ is the church, of which Christ is the head. We are to be joined together in His body (Ephesians 1:22-23; 4:15-16). Our connection to Jesus and to one another is crucial to our finding freedom and keeping that freedom.

John 15:2, "He cuts off every branch that bears no fruit, while every branch that does bear fruit, he prunes so that it will be more fruitful."

> The word "abide" is used ten times in this passage.

For many years I (Tracie) read the first part of that verse with dread and fear of being cut off from Jesus if He considered my life was unfruitful. Bruce Wilkinson in his wonderful little book, *Secrets of The Vine*, sheds light on this verse. First, the Greek word *airo* for "cut off" is more accurately translated "lift up." In trying to understand this verse, Bruce Wilkinson talked to a vinedresser, who explained to him that new branches often trail downward and grow along the ground. When they do so, their leaves become dirty and mildewed, and will never be healthy enough to grow grapes as such. The vinedresser explained that these branches were far too valuable to throw away. Rather, he washes these branches with water, lifts them up and ties them onto the trellis. Soon the formerly dirty branches thrive and produce fruit.[1]

If we are in a difficult season of our lives and there seems to be no outward signs of Christ's life, God desires to wash us with the water of His word and lift us up to where we can bask in the light of the Son. Jesus says the Father will prune us so we can produce more fruit. As a good and loving Father, God disciplines us when we sin.

Craig and I toured a vineyard to be able to better understand what Jesus was teaching in John 15. We learned that the branches produce an abundance of leaves, which must be pruned away daily. If there are too many leaves, the branches will produce little fruit because the leaves will drain the branch of the nutrients needed to grow the grapes. God desires to prune us daily of those things that drain us and inhibit growth and fruit in our lives.

God desires for us to progress from no fruit, to more fruit, to much fruit, to fruit that remains. This fruit in our lives brings glory to Him and allows others to see Christ's working in our lives. The fruit that remains is produced when we share the good news of Christ's love and freedom with others, who in turn begin bearing fruit as well.

REFLECTION
What does "abiding" look like in your everyday life?

DAY 4: The Power of Giving Thanks

Many years ago, Matthew Henry, a well-known Bible scholar, was robbed of his wallet. Knowing that the Scriptures teach us to give thanks in everything (1 Thessalonians

5:18), he meditated on this incident and recorded in his diary the following: "Let me be thankful, first, because he never robbed me before; second, because although he took my purse, he did not take my life; third, because although he took all I possessed, it was not much; and fourth, because it was I who was robbed, not I who robbed."

Power is released in our lives when we give thanks in all things. We are not instructed to give thanks "for" all things, but to give thanks "in" all things. Giving thanks keeps our focus on the Lord instead of on our problems and circumstances. Regardless of what we are facing today, let's choose to obey the Scriptures and give thanks.

Marcy grew up in a family where she experienced emotional, physical and even sexual abuse. She had received much healing in her life and had worked through forgiving those who had hurt her. The final breakthrough came when she was enabled by the grace of God to look back on her childhood and thank God for her family and that He was with her in the midst of all the pain she had endured. She could thank God because she now recognized God's hand and this love sustained her throughout her life. She also realized that she would not be who she was or where she was today without sojourning through the valleys of brokenness of her life.

> Giving thanks keeps our focus on the Lord instead of on our problems and circumstances.

In Romans 8:28 (Amplified) we read, "And we know [with great confidence] that God [who is deeply concerned about us] causes all things to work together [as a plan] for good to those who love God, to those who are called according to His plan and purpose."

In John chapter 9, Jesus and His disciples encounter a man who had been blind from birth. The disciples asked Him whose sin was to blame. Jesus answered in verse 3, "It was not because of his sins or his parents' sins. This happened so the power of God could be seen in him" (NLT). Many times we get stuck in the why or how something bad could have happened. Jesus moved the disciples past this question, saying in effect, "Watch what I am going to do!"

Jesus also said in John 5:17, "My Father is always at his work to this very day and I, too, am working." Recognizing that God has been and is now working in our lives brings us to the place of thankfulness for how He has brought freedom and maturity in our lives. We experience God in the midst of our trials and we are changed into His image!

REFLECTION
Can you identify a painful or difficult time in your life that you can look back and be thankful for what God did?

For those of us who are in the middle of hardships and pain, knowing that God is at work and that He will work together all things for good in our lives brings great encouragement. In Philippians chapter 4, Paul exhorts us not be anxious about anything, but in everything, pray with thanksgiving to God. He promises that in doing this, we will experience God's peace, which "exceeds anything we can understand" (4:7 NLT). He goes on to say that in this he has learned the "secret of being content in any and every situation" (4:12) and that he "can do all things through him who gives me strength" (4:13).

We can give thanks for the things God has brought us through, for the things He is doing presently in our lives, and in advance for the things He will do in our lives because we trust in Him.

Highway 12D

I called "hello" to my neighbor as we walked into a store, "Hey! How are you doing?"

"I'm just so disappointed with life," he replied.

A few weeks later I (Tracie) was the one who was disappointed. We had a planned a big event at our church, and my heart was bursting with anticipation of what God was going to do. I was so excited to experience God together with my spiritual family. We sent out invitations. The R.S.V.P. date came and went, with only a few responses. I personally asked people if they were coming. "Oh, when is that again?" "Oh yeah, I have the invite somewhere." "No, not coming." I was crushed. I was disappointed.

Larry and LaVerne write about the "12 D's of the Devil" in their book, When God Seems Silent, describing the progression from disappointment ultimately to destruction if we proceed through all 12 D's. These "12 D's of the Devil" are: Disappointment, Discontentment, Discouragement, Doubt, Disbelief, Disillusionment, Deception, Disobedience, Discord, Dysfunction, Despair, and Destruction. This progression begins with the disappointment of unmet expectations. Recognizing, renouncing, and resisting the "12 D's of the Devil" (the 12 stages in the enemies plan to destroy us) is critical in the life of every believer. This whole process does not happen overnight, but through small steps not unlike the proverbial frog in the kettle of water who doesn't know he is being boiled.

> Disillusionment whispered, "What is the point of any of this?"

For me, the disappointment led to discouragement. Here I was preparing for this event and at the brink of tears the entire time. "Why are we even doing this?" I asked as doubt crept in, dominating my thoughts. Even though we had believed God had shown us to do this, I wasn't so sure anymore. Disillusionment whispered, "What is the point of any of this?" "People don't even care." I began to agree with the enemy's deception and I began walling off my heart from my brothers and sisters whom I loved. Disobedience and discord was beginning to set in. Dysfunction was taking over as I made this personal, compiling a "Who's Naughty and Nice List" in my head. Delusional was not one of the original 12 D's, but I was on a roll!

I complained to my husband. I had worked myself into despair. I was flying along Highway 12 D at a dangerous speed, next stop destruction. I could have gotten off at any of the earlier possible exits, beginning with disappointment had I only gone to God, poured out my heart, dealt with my unmet expectations and extended grace and forgiveness.

Finally, I listened to my husband who had told me over and over, "Praise God for who comes. Keep your eyes on what God is doing." The night of the event, I made a decision to worship God with all my heart, thank Him for all that He had done, what He was doing this night, and what He was going to do, because everything was in His hands anyway. I repented for how far along this road I had travelled, and for the judgments I had made. He made me whole again, again.

In the book, *The Lion, the Witch, and the Wardrobe*, Peter engages in his first battle, killing a wolf with the sword Aslan gave him. Afterwards, Aslan commands Peter to clean his sword. Each of us engages in life's battles on a daily basis. We must clean ourselves from the gore of battle or our hearts will grow corroded and tarnished, just as a sword might when it is not maintained between battles. We must deal with life's disappointments.

REFLECTION
Describe the disappointments that you are dealing with.

Proverbs 4:23 instructs us to watch over our heart with all diligence, to guard it above all else. Why? Because everything we do flows from the heart and it is our heart that will determine the course of our life. When I need a heart checkup, I turn to Psalm 19:14 (NLT) and pray "May the words of my mouth and the meditation [thoughts] of my heart be pleasing to you, O Lord, my rock and my redeemer."

Quails in a Circle

DAY 6

Charles Swindoll, a well-known Bible teacher, tells the story about a covey of quails that a farmer brought to sell in a market in India. The farmer tied the leg of each quail to a stick to force them to march round and round the stick. At the market was a man, who having compassion on the poor little birds, purchased all of them. He then instructed the farmer to set them free. The farmer cut the string from each quail, yet the birds continued walking around in the same circle. The man shooed them away and they landed a few yards away, resuming their small circular march as if they were still bound.[2]

The quails had been set free, yet they continued to live exactly as before, still confined within a small circle. They were free and yet still bound. One of the most tragic things to observe is people who have chosen to follow Christ but continue to repeat their same patterns of sin. It is agonizing to watch people continue vicious cycles of sin and loss over and over again. If we are not careful, any of us can fall into this trap.

"You, my brothers and sisters, were called to be free"

(Galatians 5:13). Jesus died on the cross and rose again for our freedom. That freedom is not just in the life beyond in heaven. It is meant for your life and my life today. It is God's will that you be free now, not perpetually cycling around a stake when your shackles have been cut. "If the Son sets us free"—we are "free indeed!" (John 8:36).

Jesus taught that, "the kingdom of heaven is like a merchant seeking fine pearls, and upon finding one pearl of great value, he went and sold all that he had and bought it" (Matthew 13:44-46 NASB). Our freedom is the priceless gem found only in living in the realm of the King. We have to seek freedom in order to obtain it. I (Tracie) believe that the life we live on earth is too short not to live free. I want to appropriate all that Christ died on the Cross for me. I believe this is one of the ways I honor Him.

> They were free and yet still bound.

Several years ago Craig and I realized that we were locked into a cycle of hurting one another with our words and actions. Our unhealthy communication cycle not only affected us but also our children. We knew that we were powerless to end it by ourselves, so we spoke to those who were in leadership in our lives and followed their advice to seek ministry and counseling.

Craig and I set on a journey to let God do whatever He wanted to do in us. It involved a lot of repentance for each of our actions. We both recognized how much we were reacting out of our individual pain and the lies we had come to believe about ourselves and each other. We did a lot of forgiving and received much healing. It was a painful time, to be sure, but less painful than to keep circling around the same mountain, continuing to hurt one another. There was a cost. This season was our pearl of great price. Yet Craig and I can both say with complete confidence that we are both walking in freedom individually, resulting in a greater oneness in our marriage.

REFLECTION
What cycles keep you stuck? What keeps you from seeking freedom?

DAY 7: For Freedom

Galatians 5:1 tells us, "It is for freedom that Christ set us free." We are on a journey of freedom. God invites us to freedom. He has extended to us the invitation through Christ Jesus, but we must choose it. It is our choice. He will love us either way, but without freedom, we will never fully reach our God-given destiny and potential, and we will not have the full testimony of God's goodness to share with others who also need God's freedom. This path of freedom is a journey that will cause us to deal with our pain, our anger, our fears, our weaknesses and sins. The journey requires forgiveness, trust in God and acceptance of His perfect love. The journey may be difficult, but the destination is freedom, and freedom is worth the journey. Life is too short to not become whole and live free.

In the Old Testament, Joseph travelled this journey. As a child, he experienced the rejection and hatred of his brothers, resulting in being thrown in a pit and sold into slavery to a man named Potiphar in Egypt. Potiphar's wife attempted to seduce Joseph and when he resisted her advances, she accused him of assaulting her and he was sent to prison. After spending years in prison, Joseph's ability to interpret dreams brought him before Pharaoh. God gave Joseph the interpretation of Pharaoh's dreams of seven years of plenty preceding seven years of great famine for all of Egypt. Joseph suggested a plan to save grain during the abundance to prepare for the coming famine. As a result, Pharaoh not only released Joseph from prison, but he appointed him to be in charge of all of Egypt to implement this plan.

When the famine came, it not only affected Egypt but Canaan as well where his father and brothers live. His brothers travelled to Egypt to buy grain, and ultimately Joseph reveals himself to them as his brother. He is reunited with his family and they are saved from the famine. In Genesis 50:20, Joseph says this to his brothers after they beg his forgiveness: "Don't be afraid. Am I in the place of God? You intended to harm me, but God intended it for good to accomplish what is now being done in the saving of many lives."

> This path of freedom is a journey that will cause us to deal with our pain, our anger, our fears, our weaknesses and sins.

Joseph extended forgiveness to his brothers. He trusted God and let God form him, through all his troubles and pain into a man God could use to bring freedom from famine to many, and ensure the destiny of the further generations of the nation of Israel. Joseph did not give way to fear, temptation or destruction, but found his place in God's story of redeeming for Himself a people called by His name to love Him and to live wholeheartedly for Him.

God's dream is for you to be free. He wants to use you to help set other captives free. We encourage you to set yourself on a journey to freedom, to fight for freedom. Accept nothing less. Whatever has been your greatest weakness, your greatest pain, God wants to use as your greatest authority against the enemy and to help others find freedom. Your tests will become your testimonies to give courage to others to press on to their freedom in Christ!

REFLECTION
How can God use you to help bring His freedom to others?

Staying Free

"What joy for those whose strength
comes from the Lord,
who have set their minds on a
pilgrimage to Jerusalem.
When they walk through the Valley of Weeping,
it will become a place of refreshing springs.
The autumn rains will clothe it with blessings.
They will continue to grow stronger,
and each of them will appear before God in Jerusalem"

(Psalm 84:5-7 NLT)

Finding Freedom

Afterword

Our prayer is that you will continue to experience freedom in every area of your life. As you apply the biblical principles found in this book and walk in freedom, expect the Lord to use you to help others find freedom. Your testimony of freedom through Christ is very powerful.

Remember, insecurity tempts a person to think, "How could God ever use me? I do not know how to help anyone else find freedom. I'm afraid. I don't know the Bible well enough. I need to get my life more together."

If you feel this way, you have a lot of company, but God desires to use you to help others find freedom. Consider this: Moses complained that he could not speak properly. Jeremiah said that he was too young. Joshua was scared, but the Lord kept reassuring him to be of good courage and that he would be with him just as he was with his mentor Moses. Gideon thought he was brought up in the wrong family to be used of the Lord.

The list of excuses goes on and on. But as we trust the Lord and refuse to look at our inadequacies, we also will find the grace and strength to help others the Lord places in our lives. So many people around us need to find freedom. We have the answer to help them—through Jesus Christ! May your life and your personal God story be an example for many to find freedom and to experience wholeness in their own lives. Expect the Lord to use you! The time is now!

Larry Kreider, Tracie Nanna and Craig Nanna

Endnotes

Chapter 1
1. James Strong, *Strong's Exhaustive Concordance* (Michigan: World Publishing), 3339.
2. (www.zmescience.com, *How Caterpillars Gruesomely Turn Into Butterflies*, Tibi Puiu, January 7, 2015)
3. (http://www.ansp.org/explore/online-exhibits/butterflies/lifecycle)
4. Stasi Eldredge, *Becoming Myself* (Colorado: David C. Cook, 2013), 16.

Chapter 2
1. John Eldredge, *Waking the Dead* (Tennessee: Thomas Nelson Inc., 2003), 15.
2. Ibid., 17.
3. Derek Prince, *They Shall Expel Demons* (Michigan: Chosen Books, 1998), 14-16.
4. (https://www.thattheworldmayknow.com/gates-of-hell-article Ray Vander Laan)
5. Elisabeth Elliot, *Discipline, The Glad Surrender* (Michigan: Revell Books, 1982), 66.

Chapter 3
1. James Strong, *Strong's Exhaustive Concordance* (Michigan: World Publishing), 2398.
2. Ibid., 264.
3. Ibid., 5771.
4. Ibid., 6588.
5. Derek Prince, *Foundational Truths for Christian Living* (Florida: Charisma House, 2006), 78.
6. James Strong, *Strong's Exhaustive Concordance* (Michigan: World Publishing), 6485.
7. Gilda Radner, *It's Always Something* (New York: Avon Books, 1989), 268-269.

8. Albert Edward Winship, *Jukes-Edwards: A Study in Education and Heredity* (Pennsylvania: R.L. Myers & Co., 1900), 55, 74-86.

Chapter 4
1. Anne Lamott, *Small Victories: Spotting Improbable Moments of Grace* (New York: Penquin Books, 2014) 51.
2. Thayer and Smith, *The New American Standard New Testament Greek Lexicon* (1999), http://www.biblestudytools.com/lexicon/greek/nas/aphesis.html
3. Neil T. Anderson, *Finding Freedom from Addiction* (California: Regal Books, 1996), 314.
4. John Bevere, *Good or God?* (Colorado: Messenger International, Inc., 2015), 140.

Chapter 5
1. Kris Vallotten, *Spirit Wars* (Michigan: Chosen Books, 2012), 47-48.

Chapter 6
1. James Strong, *Strong's Exhaustive Concordance* (Michigan: World Publishing), 4265.
2. David A. Seamands, *Redeeming the Past* (Colorado: Cook Communications, 2002), 61.
3. Christine Cain, *Unashamed* (Michigan: Zondervan, 2016), 1.

Chapter 7
1. www.nbcolympics.com/video/michael-phelps-chats-bob-costas-extended-interview

Chapter 8
1. Bruce Wilkinson, *Secrets of the Vine* (Oregon: Multinomah Publishers, 2001), 33-35.
2. Charles R. Swindoll, *Day by Day with Chuck Swindoll* (Tennessee : Thomas Nelson, 2000), Week 5—Sunday.

Finding Freedom Chapter 1 Outline
The Cry For Freedom

1. **When It All Goes Wrong**
   a. When we feel powerless and not in control of our emotions and actions, there is often something deeper going on.
   b. Paul describes the battle between our sinful nature (flesh) and our inner man (spirit) in Romans 7:18-25.
   c. God offers us victory through Christ Jesus our Lord.

2. **Wasn't This All Taken Care Of At The Cross?**
   a. When we don't understand that our Christian walk is a journey, not a fixed point, we can become discouraged when we struggle and fall into old patterns of sin.
   b. The Bible tells us that we are God's handiwork (Ephesians 2:10) and that we can be confident that "he who began a good work in you will carry it on to completion in Christ Jesus," (Philippians 1:6).
   c. Our identity is not in what we do or not do, but in that we are a children of God, loved and accepted by Him.

3. **Transformed**
   a. Romans 12:2 exhorts us to be "transformed" from the pattern of this world into the image of Jesus (Romans 8:29).
   b. The obstacles to our path of transformation are (Hebrews 12:1-2): sin and the hindrances of generational sin, ungodly beliefs, hurts and wounds and strongholds.
   c. God has a plan for freedom from sin and hindrances and promises us in 2 Corinthians 3:17-18.

Teaching Outline

4. Put Off, Put On
   a. To walk in freedom and victory over sin, we must learn to put off the old self and put on the new self (Ephesians 4:22-24; Colossians 3:9; Romans 6:6-7).
   b. Galatians 5:16-23 describes the process of "putting off" and "putting on" in terms of living by the Spirit versus living by the sinful nature.

5. God Wants You to Be Free
   a. Jesus came to free us from the power of sin and death (1 John 3:8; Revelation 1:5; 1 Corinthians 15:57).
   b. When we have freedom, we are free to choose to follow and obey Him, and free to say "no" to sin in our lives.

6. Spirit, Soul and Body
   a. We are made up of spirit, soul and body (1 Thessalonians 5:23). When we are born again, our spirit is instantly reborn (John 3:3-7).
   b. Our soul, which is our mind, will and emotions, must be renewed by the truth God's Word (Romans 12:2).
   c. The Bible speaks of our body as "the flesh" or our "sinful nature" (Colossians 3:1-10).

7. Freedom from Condemnation
   a. God offers freedom from condemnation and accusations (1 John 1:9; Romans 8:1). God's conviction brings hope.
   b. Satan uses condemnation and confusion and doubt to harass us, but "God is not a God of confusion but of peace" (1 Corinthians 14:33).
   c. When we choose to believe the Word of God and refuse to live under the devil's condemnation, we will overcome the devil's accusations against us.

Finding Freedom Chapter 2 Outline
The War for Freedom

1. **We Are at War**
   a. We are in the middle of a great battle between God and Satan for the hearts of men and women.
   b. God sent Jesus to conquer sin, death and the power of Satan (Colossians 2:15) and give us life (John 10:10), yet Satan still seeks to destroy those whom God loves (1Peter 5:8).
   c. Understanding that we are at war helps us fight accordingly.

2. **Freedom from Demonic Activity**
   a. Jesus' threefold activity on earth was preaching, healing the sick and delivering people from demons (Acts 10:38; Matthew 12:28; Luke 11:28). He gave us authority to do the same (Luke 9:1; Mark 17:17).
   b. Christians cannot be possessed (Romans 8:9-11), but occult practices can lead to demonic bondage (Leviticus 19:26,31).
   c. Satan seeks to lure us away from loyalty to Christ but God's Spirit who is in you is greater than the devil" (1 John 4:4).

3. **Overcoming the Enemy**
   a. Jesus declared victory over Satan, to build His church and the "gates of hell will not overcome it" (Matthew 16:18).
   b. Jesus gives weapons to overcome the devil: the name of Jesus (Matthew 28:18; Philippians 2:10-11), the blood of Jesus and the word of our testimony (Revelation 12:11).
   c. We overcome Satan when our lives submitted to Jesus and the finished work of the Cross (Colossians 1:20; Mark 8:35).

4. **In the Middle of the Night**
   a. There is a spiritual battle for our allegiance (Ephesians 6:12).

Teaching Outline

    b. We must bring thoughts into submission to Christ (2 Cor. 10:3-5).
    c. We overcome because the same Spirit which raised Christ from the dead lives in us (Romans 8:11).

5. Strongholds
    a. A demonic stronghold is a spiritual fortress where Satan has gained access through our sin, ungodly beliefs and unhealed hurts (2 Corinthians 10:4).
    b. Strongholds are things we choose above God. Strongholds keep us from knowing God's love and keep us in bondage.
    c. God desires for us to choose to run to Him as our refuge and stronghold (Psalm 9:9; Psalm 18:2). "He gives us the victory through our Lord Jesus Christ" (1 Corinthians 15:57).

6. What Are the Schemes the Enemy Uses in Your Life?
    a. The Bible teaches us to put on the full armor of God to stand against devil's strategies (Ephesians 6:11), which pull us down and bring bondage to sin.
    b. Jesus has been tempted in every way and will provide us with a way of escape (1 Corinthians 10:13).
    c. Take a spiritual inventory to understand the enemy's schemes against your weaknesses and enact a plan to overcome.

7. Resisting the Devil
    a. Demonic spirits attempt to control us.
    b. Take authority over the devil through proclaiming God's Word and the name of Jesus (James 4:7, Matthew 12:28-29; Mark 16:17).
    c. Wholeness, emotional health and victory in every area of our lives are inheritances to His heirs and children (Galatian 3:29; Romans 8:16). He promises to give us strength to overcome (Philippians 4:13).

Finding Freedom Chapter 3 Outline
Understanding Patterns of Sin and Bondage

1. **Sin 101**
   a. Three Hebrew words describe sin.
   b. The effects of sin are separation from God, guilt and shame, broken relationships, hardened hearts and bondage to sin.
   c. We are promised in 1 John 1:7-9 that if we confess our sin, God will forgive us and purify us from all our sin.

2. **No Desire, No Hook**
   a. Satan uses our desires to tempt us and entice us into sin (James 1:13-15).
   b. It is the desires of a heart unsubmitted to Christ, which lead us to sin (James 4:1; Matthew 5:27-28; Proverbs 4:23).
   c. As we delight in Him, our desires change, become like His and the enemy can no longer entice us into sin (Psalm 37:4).

3. **Wrong Way on a One-Way Street (Repent and Renounce)**
   a. Repentance means recognizing what we are doing wrong and changing direction (Matthew 3:2,8).
   b. Repentance includes asking for forgiveness and making things right if possible.
   c. We obtain freedom from sin through repentance and renouncing our sin (2 Corinthians 4:2; Philippians 3:7-8).

4. **Generational Sin and Strongholds**
   a. Generation sins are patterns of sin passed down through generations (Exodus 20:5-6).
   b. To be free from generational sins, confess them to God and repent of them (Ezekiel 18:14-22).

c. The effects of sin can be seen to the third and fourth generations, but God shows His love to a thousand generations of those who love Him and keep His commandments.

5. **Ties That Bind**
   a. A soul tie is an attachment or a bond to another person, emotionally and spiritually.
   b. Unhealthy, unholy soul ties bind two people together.
   c. God desires for us to enjoy the benefits of being united with Him and the godly relational boundaries He has set for us (1 Corinthians 6:16-17).

6. **Breaking the Power of Sexual Bondage**
   a. God created us in His image, male and female and He declared it was good (Genesis 1:27-28).
   b. Sexual sins have great consequence in our lives because they are tied to the core of our identity (1 Corinthians 6:18-20).
   c. We can be free from sexual sin. 1 Corinthians 6:11 states, "And such were some of you. But you were washed, but you were sanctified, but you were justified in the name of the Lord Jesus and by the Spirit of our God."

7. **Putting the Pieces Back Together Again**
   a. God created sex to be pure and holy, but the enemy perverts and uses it bring pain and bondage into peoples' lives.
   b. God can restore us, putting the pieces of our heart together so that we can walk in His freedom of pure, holy love.

Finding Freedom Chapter 4 Outline
The Power of Forgiveness

1. **Two Men and a Snake**
   a. Forgiveness means to release someone of their offense toward you.
   b. It is important to understand what forgiveness really means.
   c. Unforgiveness is a trap set by the enemy; therefore, we are called to forgive (2 Corinthians 2:11-12; Colossians 3:13; Matthew 18:34-35).

2. **Forgiving God**
   a. Because of disappointments and painful experiences in life, we sometimes blame God and hold bitterness in our hearts towards Him.
   b. Through forgiving God and choosing to believe who He says He is in His Word, we can be free from bitterness and feel His love in our lives.

3. **Anger and Forgiveness**
   a. We can use anger to protect us and control those around us. However, anger also controls us and causes us to hurt those we care about.
   Ex: Tracie's struggle with anger
   b. To be free from anger controlling us: forgive those who have hurt us and choose to trust God for healing of our pain (Colossians 3:13).

4. The Power of His Grace
   a. Grace is the free and unearned favor of God. Grace also gives us the power and desire to do His will (1 Peter 5:5-6).
   b. Humility places us in a position to receive God's grace.
   c. Healthy people practice self-talk, speaking words of truth, life and grace.

5. It's All Grace
   a. The book of Galatians outlines the struggle between trusting in God's grace and striving in our own works (Galatians 3:1-5; 5:7).
   b. Understand that grace is God's empowerment for us to live for Christ.
   c. We can boast in our weaknesses, allowing the grace of Christ to work through us (2 Corinthians 12:9) and extend that same grace to others.

6. Letting Go to Reach Upward
   a. We must let go of the past in order to reach for and lay hold of the freedom that God has for us (Philippians 3:12-14).
   b. Jesus gave up His will for the Father's will: to endure the cross and secure our freedom (Philippians 2:12).

7. Finding Freedom from Painful Memories: Bell Theory
   a. Although we forgive, we often continue to deal with the painful memories.
   b. Seeking help from others can bring healing (James 5:16).
   c. Secret to finding freedom from the painful memories.
   Ex: Corrie Ten Boon and the reverberating bell.

Finding Freedom Chapter 5 Outline
Whose Voice Are You Listening to?

1. **Whose Voice Will You Follow?**
   a. We must train ourselves to listen to God's voice above all others and to shut out the voice of the enemy and his accusations.
   b. We train ourselves to know God's voice by learning His character and His ways from His Word (2 Timothy 2:15; 1 Corinthians 13; James 3:17; Psalm 101:3).
   c. When we know the Good Shepherd's voice, we will never follow a stranger (John 10:4-5).

2. **Mirror, Mirror on The Wall**
   a. Our mind can distort things, causing us to see things wrong (Jeremiah 17:9) and then jump to wrong conclusions.
   b. We filter life through these wrong conclusions based on lies and ungodly beliefs (John 8:44; Romans 12:2).
   c. Ungodly beliefs affect how we view God, ourselves and others.
   d. Each of us need a new mirror and filter.

3. **Who Do You Think You Are?**
   a. Satan continually accuses and condemns us, which brings hopelessness..
   b. God convicts but never condemns.
   c. Learn to differentiate between God's voice and the voice of the accuser.

Teaching Outline

4. **Stop Believing the Lie and Start Speaking the Truth**
   a. Words spoken over us by others can affect us for years.
   b. Allow God to speak His truth over us to become free (John 8:32).

5. **The Power of Words**
   a. Words are powerful and can bring either blessing or cursing (James 3:10).
   b. Find freedom from the power of words through forgiveness, repentance from agreement with the lies and replacing them with God's truth.

6. **Whose Report Will You Believe?**
   a. Two plans and purposes are laid out for our lives: one from God and one from Satan who seeks to destroy us (1 Peter 5:8).
   b. God has a plan for your life, to give you a future and a hope (Jeremiah 29:11-13).
   c. We choose to trust in God's plan for our lives, knowing that nothing can ever separate us from God's love (Romans 8:38-39).

7. **Not All Thoughts Are Our Own**
   a. Central to the spiritual war we are engaged in are our thoughts.
   b. Satan attacks us through planting thoughts and then accusing us of these ideas being our thoughts and desires.
   Ex: Daniel
   c. Take captive every thought and make it obedient to Christ (2 Corinthians 10:3-5).

Finding Freedom Chapter 6 Outline
Healing the Broken Heart

1. **I Saw You**
   a. When we experience pain, trauma or loss, we are vulnerable to the lies of the enemy.
   b. Satan uses anger to gain footholds in our lives (Ephesians 4:26).
   c. Our pain does not go unnoticed by God. He heals us with His love and replaces the lies with truth.

2. **Sunburn**
   a. Our hearts can be raw from our pain and brokenness and cause us to react out of that pain (James 4:1).
   b. God longs to heal the brokenhearted.
   c. If we do not look to God in our pain, we stumble in darkness, living out of that pain.

3. **Put Away Childish Things**
   a. We can become entrapped and bound by the beliefs and patterns of sin in our lives as a result of traumatic things we experienced as a child.
   b. Jesus revealed His heart towards children in Matthew 18:6-7.
   c. 1 Corinthians 13:11 exhorts us to put away childish things.

4. **Shame**
   a. Shame defines us as worthless and keeps from receiving God's love, healing and forgiveness.
   b. Shame causes us to hide and keeps us from intimacy with God and with others.
   c. We can come out of hiding, receive healing and be free from shame (1 John 1:7,9; James 5:16).

Teaching Outline

5. **Waves of Grief and Waves of Grace**
   a. Loss and grief can be overwhelming and hard to bear.
   b. The Bible tells us that there is manifold grace to match every kind of trial we go through (1 Peter 4:10; 1 Peter 1:6-7).
   c. "For of His fullness we have received grace upon grace" (John 1:16) and God comforts us in all our troubles (1 Corinthians 1:3).

6. **You Don't Have Anything to Prove**
   a. Disappointment, loss and pain can cause us to feel hopeless and incapable of doing anything valuable for God.
   b. Knowing we don't have anything to prove to God empowers us to do things we could never do in our own strength.
   c. God's power is made perfect in our weakness (1 Corinthians 12:9-10).

7. **Have You Been Dropped, Burned or Crippled?**
   a. God is calling His people who have been burned and broken.
   b. God has a plan of redemption for every believer and seeks to accomplish His plan through ordinary people like us.

Finding Freedom Chapter 7 Outline
Receiving the Father Heart of God

1. **Homecoming**
   a. In Luke 15:11-32 Jesus told the story of the Prodigal Son because He wanted us to know the heart of God the Father.
   b. Jesus leads us to our Father (John 14:9; 1 Timothy 2:5) who always loves us and waits for us with open arms.

2. **Dealing with Father Issues**
   a. Because of the lack of relationship with their mother or father, many people suffer from a love deficit that also affects their ability to give and receive love from others.
   b. We have a Father God who wants to heal our "father issues." God is Abba (daddy). We can open our hearts and trust Him today (Romans 8:15).

3. **Freedom from The Orphan Spirit**
   a. The orphan spirit is a result of experiencing abandonment, rejection or neglect from people in our lives.
   b. The orphan spirit can cause us to believe that no one, including God, could ever be trusted.
   c. We can receive healing from God through forgiving those who have hurt us and begin to define ourselves as children of God (Psalm 27:10; Psalm 68:5).

Teaching Outline

4. **Daddy's Delight**
   a. Jesus was intent on introducing mankind to His Father who is also our Father (John 14:7; John 20:17).
   b. How we view God as Father is strongly influenced by our experiences with our earthly fathers and mothers as well as authority figures in our lives.

5. **Don't Give Way to Fear**
   a. All of us experience consequences as a result of other people's actions that wounded us or compromised our wellbeing.
   b. Fear causes us to try to control our lives and drives us to go outside of God's plans and drives us to sin.
   c. We can choose to do what is right, trust God and not give way to fear (1 John 4:18; 2 Timothy 1:7; James 4:7).

6. **Healing of our Memories and Emotions**
   a. God desires to heal painful memories and our emotions.
   b. God desires to expose lies in order for us to receive healing and freedom.
   c. God desires to heal painful memories from our relationship with our parents (Psalm 27:10).
   d. Forgiveness is key to our healing (Matthew 5:14-15).

7. **From Slavery to Sonship**
   a. Many of us continue to live as if we are imprisoned by sin and our past because of shame, guilt and condemnation.
   b. Because Jesus has set us free, we are no longer slaves to fear, sin or our past (Isaiah 61:1). We are God's children.
   c. God desires to reveal to us the difference between slavery and sonship.

Finding Freedom Chapter 8 Outline
Staying Free

1. **Keep the Doors Shut!**
   a. Walking in freedom is a partnership with the Holy Spirit (Philippians 2:12).
   b. Galatians 5:1 says, "Stand fast therefore in the liberty by which Christ has made us free, and do not be entangled again with a yoke of bondage."
   c. Shut doors that pull us back to our old way of thinking.

2. **Steps to Freedom**
   a. Lasting freedom is attained by a process of steps the Lord gives us in His Word.
   b. Five biblical steps that help us find freedom

3. **Abiding in the Vine**
   a. In John 15:1-17, Jesus teaches us what it means to live our life in Him.
   b. Jesus teaches us to abide in Him,
   c. Jesus lifts us up and cleans us off if we bear no fruit.
      Ex: Bruce Wilkinson
   d. God's pruning helps us to grow fruit in our lives.

Teaching Outline

4. **The Power of Giving Thanks**
   a. Power is released in our lives when we give thanks in all things (Philippians 4).
   b. Recognizing that God has been and is now working in our lives brings us to the place of thankfulness (Romans 8:28; John 5:17).

5. **Highway 12D**
   a. If we do not deal with the disappointments of life, they can lead us to destruction.
   Ex: 12D's of the Devil
   Ex: Tracie's struggles with disapointment
   b. We must keep watch over our heart, daily and especially in battle (Proverbs 4:23; Psalm 19:14).

6. **Quails in a Circle**
   a. Sadly, many of us continue in cycles of sin and loss.
   b. We must seek freedom to obtain it (Matthew 13:44-46).

7. **For Freedom**
   a. Galatians 5:1, "It is for freedom that Christ set us free."
   b. We are on a journey for freedom. Life is too short not to live free.

Reflection journaling space

Chapter 1 **The Cry for Freedom**

Day 1 *Describe a time in your life when you felt powerless over your actions.*

How have you responded to the war going on inside you between your sinful nature (flesh) and your inner man (spirit)?

Day 2 *How does your perception change when you understand that salvation is a journey?*

How does it change things to know that God is at work in you and that He will complete the work? Isn't this good news!

Day 3 *How has God changed your life?*

What areas of your life need to continue to be transformed?

Day 4 Can you identify what things you need to "put off" as well as "put on"?

Day 5 Is there any area of your life, any sin or weakness that you believe you will never overcome?

How does knowing Jesus has restored freedom to choose change your belief toward the struggle that you are facing?

Day 6 Read Colossians 3:1-10. What do you need to do with your mind in order to be renewed?

What do you need to do in order to put to death your earthly nature?

Day 7 What is the difference between conviction and condemnation?

Have you ever experienced a lack of spiritual freedom as the result of feelings of condemnation? Explain.

How can you find freedom?

Reflection journaling space

Chapter 2 **The War for Freedom**

Day 1 *How does understanding that we are at war help you in your battles?*

How does the enemy attack your heart?

Day 2 *Name examples of ways that demons can influence or oppress people today?*

How can we cast out demons?

Day 3 *Who do you say Jesus is?*

According to Revelation 12:11, how do we overcome Satan's attacks?

Finding Freedom

Day 4 *What occupies most of your thoughts, time and resources?*

Is it possible these preoccupations are idols that sway power to influence your thoughts and actions?

How can you war spiritual battle to demolish strongholds that oppose submission to Christ?

Day 5 *Where do you run to when you feel threatened and insecure?*

How do we dismantle demonic strongholds in our lives?

Day 6 *After completing the spiritual inventory, name the scheme the enemy uses to trip you up in your walk with Christ?*

What does it mean to "put on the whole armor of God"? Take time to read through Ephesians 6:14-18.

Be certain you are fully covered by putting on the Lord Jesus Christ in each of the areas identified.

Day 7 *What happens when we resist the devil in Jesus' name?*

What does it mean to "tie up the strong man?"

Reflection journaling space
Chapter 3 **The War for Freedom**

Day 1 *Can you identify sin in your life as described above?*

How would your life change if you truly believed you were forgiven as soon as you confessed your sin to God?

Day 2 *What desires have you not surrendered to the Lord?*

What does it mean to "delight yourself in the Lord" and how can you grow in this?

Day 3 *What does it mean to repent and renounce?*

What would it look like to repent and renounce a specific sin in your life?

Day 4 *Ask the Holy Spirit to reveal to you any generational sin affecting you today.*

Trust that when you confess and repent, you will be free as well as a thousand generations to come.

Day 5 *Do you have any ungodly soul ties that hinder your walk with God and hinder you from having healthy relationships with others?*

Take time and ask the Holy Spirit to bring to your mind every ungodly soul tie that you need to bring to Him. You may want to write each name down on a piece of paper as He shows you, and then repent and break each of these soul ties in Jesus' name. Rip the paper into tiny pieces as an act of breaking each of these ties. Receive Christ's forgiveness, His freedom, His holiness, and His wholeness in your life!

Day 6 *How has sexual bondage defined your life, and what is the new identity that God wants you to define your life by now?*

Do you have any sexual bondage in your life? Take time to repent and break all unholy sexual ties in Jesus' name.

Day 7 *Do you walk in an intimate Father-child relationship with God, and in a life of holy love?*

Or, do you feel as if you have pieces of yourself scattered everywhere?

Take time to pray the prayer and allow the Father to help you become whole again in Him.

Reflection journaling space

Chapter 4 **The Power of Forgiveness**

Day 1 *Take a moment and ask the Lord to reveal to you anyone you have not forgiven.*

Lord Jesus, I choose to forgive _____ (name of the person) for _____ (name the specific sin/hurt/offense against you). Because You have freely forgiven me of my sin, I also freely forgive _____ (name of the person). I ask You to bless them today with your salvation, your healing, and your freedom. I release unforgiveness in my heart to You Lord. I am free!

NOTE: Continue to forgive others as often as necessary to be free (could be 77 times).

Day 2 *Is there anything for which you need to "forgive" the Lord?*

Do you have any bitterness or resentment toward God for allowing you to struggle through disappointment and suffering?

Day 3 *Do you "see" a future for yourself and your organization with the help of the Holy Spirit? Have you taken the necessary time to be sure of the vision and write it out?*

Day 4 *What is a definition of grace?*

How can we encourage ourselves in the Lord?

Day 5 *What is your salvation based on, your works or faith?*

What is your understanding of grace?

Day 6 *What is the Lord asking you to let go of in order to "lay hold" of the freedom that he has for you?*

What are the consequences of not letting go?

Is there a fear that has you paralyzed?

Day 7 *Explain how the bell theory works.*

Do you struggle with painful memories? Are you ready to be set free?

Reflection journaling space
Chapter 5 **Whose Voice Are You Listening To?**

Day 1 *Whose voices do you listen to the most?*
How can you learn to recognize God's voice?

Day 2 *Can you recall a time when you reached a wrong conclusion?*
Can you identify any ungodly beliefs through which you are filtering life?

Day 3 *Recall times when you heard Satan accuse you and when you sensed God convicting you. How did you respond?*
How can you discern the difference between condemnation and conviction?

Day 4 *What is the lie that has become an ungodly belief in your life?*
What is God's truth to replace that lie and set you free?

Day 5 *Have you had hurtful words spoken over you?*

Have these words turned into lies that you have accepted as truth?

Today you can break agreement with them and replace them with God's truth.

Day 6 *Explain the difference between God's plan and the enemy's plan.*

Ask God to show you both so that you can pursue His wonderful plan and combat the enemy's.

Memorize a scripture that proclaims God's plan for your life.

Day 7 *What does knowing that every thought you think doesn't originate with you mean to you?*

When we are weak where can we go from attacks in our thoughts?

Reflection journaling space
Chapter 6 **Healing the Broken Heart**

Day 1 *Can you remember a time of pain, trauma or loss in which you made an agreement with the enemy?*

Ask God to bring healing to that memory and to give you His truth to replace the lie.

Day 2 *Can you identify the wounds of your heart and your reaction to them?*

What are your thoughts, emotions and reactions trying to tell you?

How might you be trying to protect and comfort yourself rather than trusting in God?

Day 3 *Can you think of any pain from your past (specifically childhood) that has caused patterns of sin or unhealthy behaviors in your life?*

Are you willing to ask Jesus to heal your pain and put away ungodly beliefs and sin from your childhood?

Day 4 *Are you hiding?*

Can you identify how your shame affects your relationship with God and with others?

Are you ready to come into the light?

Day 5 *Are you grieving?*

What does it mean to know that there is a grace for every grief you encounter in life?

Day 6 *Can you identify anything that you are trying to prove to God, to others?*

How different would your life be if you truly believed that you didn't have anything to prove?

Day 7 *Have you ever experienced feeling dropped? Explain.*

What is the lie Mephibosheth lived under?

How did he find freedom?

Reflection journaling space

Chapter 7 Receiving the Father Heart of God

Day 1 *What would it be like if you truly believed that God's arms were open wide to you and His delight was in you?*

What is keeping you from believing that?

Will you let Jesus lead you home to your Father God?

Day 2 *How can "father issues" affect your ability to give and receive love?*

How does Father God want to minister to your heart cry for love?

Day 3 *Do any behaviors in your life reveal that you are dealing with an orphan spirit?*

Are you willing to forgive others who have rejected you, open your heart to the Father's love, and to be loved by a church family?

Day 4 *Take some time to prayerfully consider the following: How do you perceive God?*

How does God want to reveal Himself to you?

Day 5 *What fear(s) do you live with?*
How do you typically "give way" to fear?
What are you trying to control in your life?

Day 6 *Are there any parental wounds in your life that need to be healed?*

What can hinder us from being healed of painful memories?

Day 7 *In what ways do you still live behind the prison doors of sin and your past?*

As you take time to pray through the Scriptures above, ask the Father to take you on the journey out of slavery into sonship with Him.

Reflection journaling space
Chapter 8 **Staying Free**

Day 1 *How is the enemy trying to rob you of your freedom in Christ?*
What doors in your life do you need to shut?

Day 2 *What are five steps we can take to find freedom?*
Where do you see yourself in these five steps?

Day 3 *What does "abiding" look like in your everyday life?*
How is your fruit production?
In what areas of your life does God desire to wash, lift up and prune you?

Day 4 *Can you identify a painful or difficult time in your life that you can look back and be thankful for what God did?*
Explain the power of giving thanks. How does this apply to your life?

Day 5 *Describe the disappointments that you are dealing with. Are you willing to repent of all words, thoughts or actions that are not pleasing to God?*

Will you let God search your heart and bring healing as only He can?

Day 6 *What cycles keep you stuck?*

What keeps you from seeking freedom?

What are you willing to do to seek your freedom?

Day 7 *How can you continue to fight for your freedom?*

How can God use you to help bring His freedom to others?

Larry Kreider

Larry Kreider serves as International Director of DOVE International, a network of churches throughout the world. For more than three decades, DOVE has used the New Testament "house to house" strategy of building the church with small groups.

As founder of DOVE International, Larry initially served for 15 years as senior pastor of DOVE Christian Fellowship in Pennsylvania, which grew from a single small group to more than 2,300 believers in 10 years. Today, DOVE believers meet in more than 400 congregations and in thousands of small groups in five continents of the world.

In 1971, Larry helped establish a youth ministry that targeted unchurched youth in northern Lancaster County, Pennsylvania. DOVE grew out of the ensuing need for a flexible New Testament-style church that could assist these new believers.

Larry and his wife LaVerne teach worldwide and encourage believers to reach out from house to house, city to city and nation to nation, and empower and train others to do the same.

Larry writes for Christian periodicals and has written 40 books that have sold more than 500,000 copies, with many translated into other languages. Larry earned his Masters of Ministry with a concentration on leadership from Southwestern Christian University. He and his wife have been married 45 years and live in Lititz, Pennsylvania. They enjoy spending time with their four amazing children, two sons-in-law, a daughter-in-law and six amazing grandkids.

Read Larry's blog at www.dcfi.org/blog
Like Larry and LaVerne Kreider on Facebook
Follow Larry Kreider on Twitter

Craig and Tracie Nanna

Craig and Tracie Nanna serve as lead pastors of TransformChurch, a multi-cultural, inner-city church that they planted twenty years ago in Reading, Pa. Craig and Tracie met at Oral Roberts University, where they both graduated with theology degrees and have since served in various ministry roles.

Together, the couple serve on the DOVE USA Apostolic Team, and share a longing to see the church of America experience the Greatest Awakening. As the director for DOVE Latin America, Craig carries a heart to see a greater church planting movement in that region. Tracie enjoys ministering around the world to see God's kingdom advance, healthy leaders raised up and God's people set free. In her role as LifeGroup and Discipleship Pastor at TransformChurch, Tracie seeks to equip every believer to know how to be a disciple of Christ. Through her book, *Walking with Jesus*, believers learn how to fulfil the Great Commission.

During twenty-five years of extensive ministry, Craig and Tracie observe many believers who are stunted in spiritual growth and struggle with the brokenness of their pasts. As a result, the Nannas developed the Freedom Seminar, which helps believers be healed from the pain of their pasts and set free from bondages of sin.

Craig and Tracie celebrated their 25th wedding anniversary. They love cheering on their three adult children who are stepping into God's calling. The Nannas enjoy traveling, especially if they have a chance to use their limited knowledge of Spanish, *la lengua celestial*.

Stay connected at www.transformchurch.church
Read Craig's blog at craignanna.wordpress.com.

Other books in this series

When God Seems Silent
Discovering His purposes in times of confusion and darkness

Why does it sometimes feel like God is silent? Is He hiding from us? Is He angry? Larry and LaVerne Kreider help us examine these questions and many of the barriers that can block the voice of God in our lives. They also reveal their own struggle with God's silences and the tremendous breakthroughs that can be discovered. *By Larry and LaVerne Kreider, 208 pages:* $12.99

Straight Talk to Leaders
What we wish we had known when we started

Four Christian leaders disclose key leadership lessons they have learned through forty years of pastoring and establishing worldwide ministries. This illuminating book explores topics such as team building, boundaries, transitions, unity, stress management, learning from criticism, making tough decisions and much more! *By Larry Kreider, Sam Smucker, Barry Wissler and Lester Zimmerman, 204 pages:* $12.99

Battle Cry for Your Marriage
Discovering breakthroughs for today's challenges

With raw honesty four couples tackle issues of spiritual, emotional and sexual intimacy along with many other marital stresses. The authors reveal marriage lessons learned through years of experience and from counseling others. Join the battle cry for healthy marriages in this generation. Biblically-based insights will inspire spouses to face issues, communicate honestly, find life-changing strategies and—most of all—love the One who gave them the gift of each other *By Larry and LaVerne Kreider, Steve and Mary Prokopchak Duane and Reyna Britton, Wallace and Linda Mitchell, 204 pages:* $12.99

**www.h2hp.com
Call 800.848.5892**

Walking with Jesus

A guide for a one-on-one discipling relationship and fulfilling the Great Commission through relational discipleship. *Walking With Jesus* provides a plan for discipleship: lessons arranged with a clear time frame, about six weeks. Designed to be used one-on-one or in a small group setting. *By Tracie Nanna*, 44 pages: **$4.99**

Biblical Foundation Series

This series by Larry Kreider covers basic Christian doctrine. Practical illustrations accompany the easy-to-understand format. Use for small group teachings (48 outlines), in mentoring relationship or as a daily devotional. *By Larry Kreider, Each book has 64 pages:* **$4.99** each, 12 Book Set: **$39**
Available in Spanish and French.

Titles in this series:
1. **Knowing Jesus Christ as Lord**
2. **The New Way of Living**
3. **New Testament Baptisms**
4. **Building For Eternity**
5. **Living in the Grace of God**
6. **Freedom from the Curse**
7. **Learning to Fellowship with God**
8. **What is the Church?**
9. **Authority and Accountability**
10. **God's Perspective on Finances**
11. **Called to Minister**
12. **The Great Commission**

The Cry for Spiritual Mothers and Fathers

Returning to the biblical truth of spiritual parenting is necessary so believers are not left fatherless and disconnected. Learn how loving, seasoned spiritual fathers and mothers help spiritual children reach their full potential in Christ. *By Larry Kreider, 224 pages*: $14.99

Your Personal House of Prayer

Christians often struggle with their prayer lives. With the unique "house plan" developed in this book, each room corresponding to a part of the Lord's Prayer, your prayer life is destined to go from duty to joy! Includes a helpful Daily Prayer Guide. *By Larry Kreider, 192 pages:* $12.99

www.h2hp.com
Call 800.848.5892